of
Oxfordshire

A County Guide
to the Unusual
by
Edward Gill

K1-L

S.B. Publications

By the same author:–
Nelson and the Hamiltons on Tour
Curiosities of South Wales
(co-author with E.C. Freeman):
Nelson and the Hamiltons in Wales and Monmouthshire

**To celebrate the birth of
our dear granddaughter, Stephanie
(27 May, 1994)**

First published in 1995 by S.B. Publications
c/o 19 Grove Road, Seaford, East Sussex BN25 1TP

ISBN 1 85770 073 2

Typeset, printed and bound by MFP Design & Print,
Longford Trading Estate, Thomas Street, Stretford, Manchester M32 0JT

CONTENTS

Front Cover: Sundial, All Souls' College, Oxford.
Back Cover: Sundial signpost, Wroxton (left); Lock-up, Wheatley (right).
Title Page: Bench end carving, Swinbrook Church.

INTRODUCTION

I first came to Oxfordshire almost forty years ago. My frequent visits were to do with business, and as much of my work was done in the evenings, I often found myself with time to spare during the day. This gave me opportunities denied to most people, to spend many hours looking at churches, visiting museums and colleges, and going round stately homes.

Fresh from industrial Lancashire's inhospitable moors, criss-crossed by crumbling black stone walls, I was enchanted by Oxfordshire's gentle landscape. Its fertile fields neatly divided by walls of mellow Cotswold stone were different; so too were its villages. In contrast to rows of smoke-blackened terraces, here there were picturesque villages with lovely old churches of stone that shone in the sun.

I began to form habits that have stayed with me for almost four decades. I could never pass an interesting building, a church or a country house, without giving way to the urge to explore it. Blenheim Palace was among the first on my list. Hardly anyone seemed to visit it then; certainly not in the week, even though the cost was only two shillings. In Oxford, the colleges captured my interest, especially the sumptuous dining halls and chapels, where the evensong I sang as a choirboy in a north Shropshire village church, took on a new and deeper meaning.

Oxfordshire is a county of contrasts. Giant cooling towers dominate Didcot, home of the Railway Museum. A few miles distant is fashionable Henley where the Royal Regatta is held every year. To the North is Shakespeare country, and flowing out of Gloucestershire in the West, is the tranquil Windrush, meandering unhurried past Burford church. Here Cromwell imprisoned rebellious troops, and on the wall outside, a sad memorial marks the place where their leaders were shot.

Visitors come from all over the world to enjoy the unique character of Oxfordshire. Few places in Britain can boast the wealth of history so carefully preserved in great houses, humble cottages, churches, colleges, and ancient sites like the strange white horse that gallops across the hill at Uffington.

Here, I have used the word 'curiosity' in its broadest sense to describe objects and places of unusual architectural and historical interest. Access to many of them is free and unrestricted, but some are privately owned, and you are asked to respect their privacy. Sometimes access is restricted, particularly where English Heritage or the National Trust are in charge, and I have endeavoured to indicate where this is so. It is by no means a definitive guide to the curiosities in the area; there are many more. It should, however, provide a wide and varied selection for visitors, and give you an unusual day out. It might even persuade local residents to take a fresh look at some of the interesting objects that are sometimes taken for granted.

Edward Gill

ACKNOWLEDGEMENTS

My thanks are due to the many authors, known and unknown, of church guides, that are such useful and reliable sources of information. Also the Oxfordshire County Libraries and in particular, the staff of the Centre for Oxfordshire Studies. In thanking the libraries, I wish to include the many public libraries beyond the bounds of Oxfordshire, that are such invaluable sources of information and knowledge to authors, students and the public at large. Long may they continue to serve our nation! I also wish to thank Lord Mostyn's Forester, Mr. Richard Davies, for providing me with the story of 'Lady', and Mr. Michael Sagar of 'Hounds' magazine for the picture of the hound with her puppies. Also Mr. Daniel Grist, Secretary of Henley Royal Regatta, for the photographs of Temple Island. I must record also, my thanks to those worthy custodians of our national inheritance, English Heritage, and in its centenary year, the National Trust. Finally I want to thank my friend Michael Bacon, who is also a firm friend of Oxfordshire, and an old boy of Magdalen's famous Choir School, for taking on the laborious task of proof reading my script.

Open-air stone pulpit, Magdalene College.

OXFORD

THE MARTYRS' MEMORIAL

Location: St. Giles'.

One of the first important monuments you see on entering Oxford from the north is the Martyrs' Memorial in St. Giles'. It was erected in 1841-43 to commemorate three 16th century Protestant Martyrs; Hugh Latimer, Bishop of Worcester, and Nicholas Ridley, Bishop of London, who were tried as heretics and burnt at the stake in 1555, and Thomas Cranmer, Archbishop of Canterbury, a fellow heretic who suffered the same fate a year later. Designed by Sir George Gilbert Scott, the memorial is based on the 13th century Eleanor Cross at Waltham in Essex. Statues of the martyrs look down on the people below; Cranmer holding his Bible bearing the significant date May 1541, to commemorate the first year of its circulation by Royal Authority. Beneath Cranmer's statue is the inscription:

'To the Glory of God and in grateful commemoration of His servants, Thomas Cranmer, Nicholas Ridley, Hugh Latimer, Prelates of the Church of England, who near this spot yielded their bodies to be burned, bearing witness to the sacred truths which they had affirmed and maintained against the errors of the Church of Rome, and rejoicing that to them it was given not only to believe in Christ, but also to suffer for His sake; this monument was erected by public subscription in the year of our Lord God MDCCCXLI.'

OXFORD

ST. MARTIN'S TOWER

Location:	Carfax Oxford.
Access:	Open daily March to October. For a small charge visitors may go to the top of the tower to get a fine view down the High Street.

Since 1032, the church of St. Martin stood at Oxford's busy cross-roads known as Carfax. Centuries of burials undermined its foundations, and in 1820 the old church was declared unsafe and pulled down. A new church was built on the site, but this too was demolished in 1896, and only the 13th century west tower, known as Carfax Tower survived. Beneath its clock, two quaint quarter boys holding hammers stand on either side of a pair of bells which they strike each quarter hour. These are replicas of the two originals now in the Museum of Oxford.

In the 14th century, the height of the tower was raised, but later lowered, following complaints from the University of townsmen throwing stones and firing arrows from it during Town & Gown disputes. The bells of St. Martin's, said to rival those of the University Church of St. Mary, were rung to summon the people of Oxford to Carfax for important announcements. New kings and queens are still proclaimed from the tower, and until last century, a curfew bell was rung each day at 4am and 8pm. In 1545 a seat beneath a lead roof was erected by the east wall of the church, for official use on special occasions. Many distinguished visitors were received here, including Queen Elizabeth I and James I. It was commonly known as the Penniless Bench, and became a place where people gathered to socialise and debate. But it attracted unruly elements, and students were forbidden to loiter there. It was considered a public nuisance, and finally demolished in 1750.

OXFORD

WHERE THREE PROTESTANTS WERE MARTYRED

Location: Broad Street.

On the 16th October 1555, Hugh Latimer and Nicholas Ridley were taken in a procession from their prison cells to a ditch outside the City's northern wall. Both were burnt at the stake in a raging fire. Cranmer, who was also under sentence, was forced to watch from a parapet on the City wall. On the 21st March 1556, he too was taken to the same place and burnt at the stake. The site on which the martyrs died is in Broad Street, opposite Balliol College. A plaque on the wall outside the college records the historic event, which is also marked by stones set in the road in the shape of a cross. The heat of the fire was so intense, that it scorched the gates which now hang in a corner of the college front Quad. While awaiting execution, the three were imprisoned in the 13th century Bocardo which stood by North Gate. The Bocardo and North Gate were demolished in 1771, but the door of Cranmer's cell has been preserved in the tower of St. Michael at the North Gate, which is open to visitors.

The cross in the road on Broad Street, marking the spot where the Martyrs died.

OXFORD

HOUSE OF EDMUND HALLEY – ASTRONOMER ROYAL

> *Location:* 7 New College Lane.
>
> *Access:* Can be viewed from outside.

A simple wooden plaque on the front of a modest town house in New College Lane, records:

> *Edmund Halley*
> *Savilian Professor of Geometry 1703-1742*
> *lived and had his observatory in this house.*

Halley has been described as the greatest English astronomer, and although he was Astronomer Royal with a long and distingushed academic career, to most people, his name is synonymous with the comet that bears his name. Long before the age of micro-chips and computers, he expended immense time and energy computing the orbits of twenty four comets. Finding three almost identical, he was convinced that the comets of 1531, 1607 and 1682, were one and the same, appearing at intervals of approximately 76 years. This same comet can be seen on the Bayeux Tapestry. The comet appeared only once during Halley's long life – in 1682, the year of his marriage. He predicted it would next appear in 1758, and on Christmas night of that year, the comet was seen in the sky. Forecasting its return, he appealed '. . . to candid posterity to acknowledge that this was first discovered by an Englishman.' His appeal was honoured, and henceforth it was known as Halley's Comet. It last appeared in 1986.

OXFORD

THE BRIDGE OF SIGHS

Location:	Hertford College, New College Lane.
Access:	Limited public access to College 9.30am to dusk.

Visitors to Venice will know how expensive it is these days, to float romantically on a gondola under the famous Bridge of Sighs. In Oxford, you can walk, or as many do, cycle beneath it. Perhaps not so romantic as a gondola, but at least it is free of charge. Reminiscent of its Venetian namesake, it was designed by Sir Thomas Jackson and erected in 1914 to link the north and south sides of Hertford College. It was here that Hertford graduate Evelyn Waugh set *Brideshead Revisited*, portraying undergraduate life in the 1920s.

OXFORD

TOWER OF THE FIVE ORDERS

Location: Opposite the Bodleian Library in The Schools Quadrangle.

Access: Quadrangle open daily.

Among Oxford's great wealth of architecture, the Tower of the Five Orders in the Schools Quadrangle must rank with the most unusual. It was the brainchild of Thomas Bodley, founder of the great library that bears his name. The tower, set on the east side of the Quadrangle takes its name from the five styles of classical columns – Tuscan, Doric, Ionic, Corinthian and Composite, which stand one above the other on the front of the building. Sheltering beneath an elaborately carved canopy on the face of the Tower is a statue of King James I, and above him the arms of the Stuarts. Work on its construction started on the day of Bodley's funeral in 1613 and was completed in 1624. It is a truly remarkable building, and a worthy monument to a great man.

OXFORD

THE SHELDONIAN THEATRE

Location:	Broad Street.
Access:	10am-12.30pm & 2-4.30pm (winter 3.30pm).

Most people only see the Sheldonian Theatre from the outside, but visitors to Oxford will be well rewarded if they take a look at its impressive interior. Capable of seating 2000, it was commissioned by Chancellor Gilbert Sheldon, who chose his young friend, Christopher Wren as the architect. Since its opening in 1669, it has been the scene of many historic University ceremonies. It was even once used for Parliament. The magnificent ceiling, painted on 32 canvas panels by Robert Streeter, sergeant painter to Charles I, gives the illusion of looking through an open roof to the sky. If you climb the stairs to the cupola, you actually walk across the top of the ceiling, and will surely be impressed by the complex network of massive timbers supporting the roof. The cupola provides impressive and unusual views of colleges and other important buildings, so be sure to take your camera!

Generations of visitors have puzzled over the identity of the sculptured heads on the railings outside the Sheldonian. Speculation as to whether they are Roman Emperors, Greek Philosophers or even the Twelve Apostles continues to this day. There might be a clue to their identity in the original building accounts in which they are described as 'termains', indicating a link with the Roman god Terminus. But the suggestion that the Greeks would have called them Herms after Hermes, the god who was placed at the entrances to temples might not be far off the mark. Whoever they were meant to be, their real identity remains a mystery. The originals, put there by Wren's master mason William Byrd, became weather-worn and were replaced in 1868, and again in the 1970s.

OXFORD

MAGDALEN COLLEGE TOWER

Location:	Magdalen College, High Street (The High).
Access:	College open to public October – March: 2-6pm. April 1-24: 12 noon – 6pm. April 25 – June 17: 2-6pm weekdays. Saturdays & Sundays 12 noon – 6pm 18th June – 30th Sept.

Visitors entering Oxford from an easterly direction will almost certainly do so by way of Magdalen Bridge. It provides a memorable first impression, dominated by the beautiful mellow stone bell tower of Magdalen (pronounced Maudlen) College. Charles I thought it '. . . the most absolute building in Oxford.' Work on the tower began in 1492, and the first bells were hauled up to their chamber in 1505. By 1509 the tower was completed at a cost of £500. For two years during construction the future Cardinal Wolsey was Bursar, and Henry VII provided timely financial help by granting the College a tax rebate. From this same tower, Royalist troops of Charles I defended Magdalen Bridge in the Civil War, by raining rocks onto the heads of Cromwell's men.

On-going renovations have taken place over the centuries, but in 1975, structural reports revealed that much of the masonry was in a perilous state and in need of urgent remedial work. The cost was estimated at £3 million, and many tons of stone were needed. The tons of local stone used in the original building were no longer available, so the builders had to turn to France, where an ample supply was found at Lorraine, in quarries used by the Romans. Scarce English Clipsham stone was used to replace the pinnacles and 144 gargoyles and heads round the top of the tower.

In accordance with age old tradition, the choir of Magdalen College ascend the tower at 6am on May Day Morning. From there they greet the coming of spring with 'Te Deum Patrem Collimus' and other hymns. On Magdalen Bridge and in The High, thousands gather to rejoice and listen. Young undergraduates celebrate in their own high-spirited way with May morning picnics in punts massed side-by-side on the river below.

Magdalen College and Tower.

OXFORD

EARL DANBY'S DORIC GATE

Location:	Botanic Gardens, High Street (The High).
Access:	The Botanic Gardens open daily 9am – 5pm.
	Admission to the gardens is free, but donations are welcomed.

The Botanic Gardens are a fitting memorial to Henry Danvers, Earl Danby, who founded The Oxford Physic Garden in 1621, as part of the School of Medicine. It was England's first physic garden, for which the Earl's head gardener, Jacob Bobart travelled the length and breadth of Europe to collect rare seeds. The gardens are entered through the Doric arch known as the Danby Gate. It was built in 1632, by Inigo Jones' master mason Nicholas Stone. He commemorated Henry Danvers with a bust in a niche above the arch, and filled the alcoves on each side, with full length statues of Charles I and Charles II, dressed as Roman Emperors.

OXFORD

THE BULLDOG INN

Location:	St. Aldate's Street.
Access:	Normal licensing hours.

The sign of The Bulldog Inn is of an undergraduate sprinting along a city street, hotly pursued by a man in a bowler hat. He is not fleeing from any ordinary man, but from a dreaded Bulldog. This is the name given by students to the University Proctors (i.e. 'policemen') responsible for imposing student discipline. The very sight of one could strike terror into the heart of an undergraduate. Not surprising when records relate that in the mid 17th-century, they were armed with arquebus – a kind of blunderbuss on a tripod; but in later years they just carried staves. In his recent autobiography, writer and M.P., Julian Critchley, describes the Bulldogs at Oxford where he was an undergraduate. 'Parties in dark suits and bowler hats, capable, so we were told, of a surprising turn of speed.' Their distinctive bowler hats are a relatively modern form of headgear; previously they wore toppers, and before that tricorn hats.

The building that houses the Bulldog Inn dates from 1380 when it was known as the Christopher Inn. In the 18th century it was converted to a coaching inn, and was a welcome stop on the busy London to Gloucester route. It was renamed The Bulldog in 1965.

OXFORD

SUNDIAL – ALL SOULS' COLLEGE

Location:	High Street.
Access:	Open Monday to Friday 2-4pm.

The large circular sundial at All Souls' was designed by Sir Christopher Wren at about the same time as he was made a Fellow of the College in 1653. It was initially placed on the Chapel wall in the First Quad, but later removed to its present site on the Codrington Library wall in the North Quad. Wren expressed himself well pleased with its accuracy – 'one may see to a minute what it is o'clock, the minutes being depicted on the sides of the rays.' The Arms of the College are in the centre of the dial, surrounded by Roman numerals indicating the hours. The motto in Latin from Martial's Epigrammata reads – PEREVNT ET IMPVTANTVR – '(The hours) pass away and are set down to (our) charge.'

OXFORD

SUNDIAL – CORPUS CHRISTI COLLEGE

Location:	Merton Street.
Access:	Open to the public 1.30-4pm.

This sundial is quite different from All Souls', being mounted on a stone cylindrical column. It is popularly known as the Pelican, because it is surmounted by a very fine pelican with outstretched wings, vulning (wounding) herself (to feed her young). A similar pelican appears on the College Arms as a symbol of piety.

It is more correctly known as the Turnbull Dial, having been made by Charles Turnbull between 1579 and 1581. Since then it has undergone numerous renovations, the first being in 1605. It was renovated again in 1625, and in 1706 was completely dismantled to be rebuilt on a large plinth. This increased its height to catch the sun's rays even in winter. During the 19th century, this lovely sundial seems to have fallen into a sad state of disrepair, and by 1873, it was in need of serious restoration. It was repainted in 1936, and completely restored and repainted in 1976, when historic documents and photographs from the College archives were used to ensure authenticity.

OXFORD

THE TALE OF THE SILVERSMITH'S DOG

Location: 131 High Street.

There was a time in England when a shop could be identified by the sign hanging over its door. The barber's pole, the three golden balls outside a pawnbroker's shop and a riding boot above the door of the shoemaker's. Such signs are much less common today; but there are still a few to be seen, and Oxford seems to have its share. A good example is the bishop's mitre over the entrance of the Mitre Hotel in The High, and opposite, a large dog holding a watch in his mouth, above the silversmiths, Payne & Son. Their business started in 1790 at Wallingford, and opened its Oxford shop in 1888. Still in the hands of the founding family, the firm has an enviable global reputation for its knowledge of modern and antique silver.

OLD HEADINGTON

THE TOMBSTONES OF OLD JOHN YOUNG – 1688

Location:	St. Andrew's churchyard, Old Headington, 3 miles east of Oxford.
Access:	Open to the public.

Tombstones of all ages throughout the country have always proved possible sources of curiosity. Oxfordshire is not without its share of eccentric memorials, some of which are featured in this book. Two of particular interest are to be found in St. Andrew's churchyard at Old Headington. They record the death of John Young who loyally supported King Charles I during the Civil War. One inscription reads:

> *'HERE LYETH JOHN*
> *WHO TO YE KING DID BELONG,*
> *HE LIV'D TO BE OLD*
> *AND YET DYED YOVNG'*

His other tombstone which stands back to back with the one above reads:

'IN MEMORY OF JOHN YOVNG WHO DYED NOV.YE 19 1688 AGED 100 YEARS'

BINSEY

ST. MARGARET'S WELL

Location:	Binsey Village.

Though Binsey is just on the edge of Oxford, the setting is delightfully rural. It is located about a mile off the busy main road that takes you from the city centre towards Botley. Turn right down Binsey Lane, and as soon as you cross the single-track bridge you are lost in a rural idyll. The Perch is the local thatch-roofed inn, where good food and fine ale are served at the bar.

Hidden among trees down a narrow lane a little way beyond the inn is the tiny 12th century church of St. Margaret of Antioch. To the rear, at the west end of the church, is Saint Margaret's Well. According to legend, the Saxon Princess Ffrediswyde, who wanted to be a nun, hid in a nearby wood to escape a pursuing suitor. The unfortunate man was struck blind when he took hold of her hand, whereupon the distressed princess prayed to St. Margaret for a cure. Water gushed from the ground on which the well stands, and his blindness was cured. The princess became St. Ffrediswyde, and pilgrims in the Middle Ages went first to her tomb in Austin Abbey, before going to the well at Binsey. Royal pilgrims included King Henry VIII and Queen Catherine of Aragon.

In medieval Oxfordshire, holy medicinal springs were known as 'treacle wells'. This one was mentioned by Lewis Carroll in *Alice's Adventures In Wonderland.*

CUMNOR

LORD LEICESTER'S QUEEN

Location:	Cumnor Village Church.
Access:	Open during normal church hours.

One thing is certain about English village churches; you never quite know what surprises await you inside. St. Michael's at Cumnor proves the point; from the moment you pass through the 14th century north door (still on its original hinges) you are confronted by numerous objects of interest. The first surprise on entering, is to come face to face with a magnificent life-size statue of Elizabeth I. Carved in Caen stone, it stares straight ahead from its plinth. Bejewelled and resplendent as befits a monarch, she holds an orb and sceptre to survey the church and scrutinise all who enter. The statue is thought to have been commissioned during the Queen's reign by her favourite, Lord Leicester, who it is said, served his Queen well.

CUMNOR

A CHAINED BIBLE AND A JACOBEAN PULPIT

In the nave, a handsomely-carved 17th century pulpit stands above a clerk's stall. Those who know about these things, seem to think it is older than the pulpit, and might be a rare survival of the Elizabethan reading pew, introduced so that priests could conduct the services in full view of the congregation. Housed in a glass-topped desk to the side of the stall is a rare chained Authorised 1611 First Edition of the King James Bible.

SPIRAL STAIRS TO THE BELFRY

Another curious object of interest is the oak spiral staircase in the bell tower. Clearly carved on its central pillar are the makers' initials and the date it was built 'T.B. G.N. 1685'. The stairs wind up to the bell chamber which houses a peal of bells dating from 1617. On the walls of the tower, plaques commemorate notable bellringing achievements.

STANTON HARCOURT

STANTON HARCOURT MANOR

Location:	Stanton Harcourt on B4449, 9 miles west of Oxford.
Access:	The Manor & Gardens are open to the public on certain Thursdays and Sundays from April to September and on Bank Holidays. For details telephone 01365-881928.

The Manor of Stanton was brought into the Harcourt family as the dowry of Isabel de Camville on her marriage to Robert de Harcourt in the middle of the 12th century. Built between 1380-1470, it was one of the earliest unfortified manor houses in England. Of the original house, the octagonal roofed Great Kitchen of 1380 and the square tower now known as Pope's Tower of 1470, have survived. The Great Kitchen is unique in England; having no chimneys, the smoke from the two open fires and ovens collected in the roof, from where it was expelled by opening wooden louvres. The louvres were operated from a parapet reached by spiral stairs rising from a corner of the kitchen.

Pope's Tower acquired its name following its occupation by the poet, Alexander Pope from 1717-1718. In a panelled room above the chancel of the chapel, lent to him by Lord Harcourt, he worked on his translation of the Iliad. For posterity, he scratched a message on a window pane, which reads: 'In the year 1718, I Alexander Pope finished here the fifth volume of Homer.' In a letter to the Duke of Buckingham, Pope describes a decaying house at the time of his stay. He portrays it as 'disjointed' having been 'built before rules were in fashion.' He goes on to describe the 'venerable tower', in which he lodged, as '. . . so like that of the church just by, that the jackdaws build in it as if it were the true steeple. Indeed, we owe this old house the same kind of gratitude that we do to an old friend who harbours us in his declining condition, nay, even in his last extremities. Anyone who sees it will own I could not have chosen a more likely place to converse with the dead. I had been mad indeed if I had left your Grace for any one but Homer.' The house must have been in a pretty poor state, for he says it was inhabited by elderly rats whose main source of subsistence was the few remaining books in the library. Happily the house is in a much better shape today, and hopefully, the books survived the rats.

STANTON HARCOURT

HENRY TUDOR'S STANDARD AND ITS BEARER

Location: Harcourt Chapel, Stanton Harcourt Church.

Access: Church open to the public.

The Harcourt Chapel was built during the reigns of Henry VI and Edward IV. It contains the tombs of generations of Harcourts, the oldest being that of Sir Robert Harcourt K.G., and his wife Margaret, in the south-east corner, to the right of the Altar. He was killed in 1471, by the Staffords of the Lancastrian Party. But the tomb that demands our attention is that of his grandson Sir Robert Harcourt K.B., on the other side of the Altar. Armoured for battle, he lies alone on a tomb that bears the Tudor Rose. Above him hang the remains of the standard he carried for Henry Tudor at the Battle of Bosworth on the 22nd August 1485. It was a battle that claimed the life of Richard III, and set the Tudors firmly on the throne of England.

It is interesting to note that Sir Robert Harcourt and his near neighbour Lord Francis Lovel of Minster Lovell, were on opposing sides at Bosworth. Sir Robert returned triumphant to Stanton Harcourt, while Lord Francis was forced to a life of obscurity and an uncertain fate.

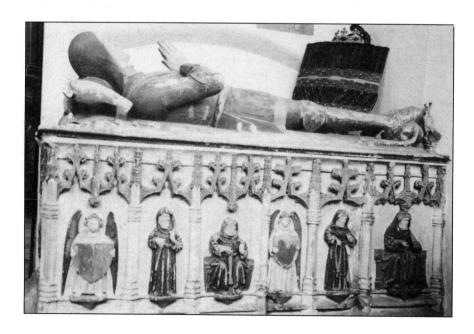

STANTON HARCOURT

A TRAGIC MEMORIAL TO YOUNG LOVERS KILLED BY LIGHTNING

Location: Stanton Harcourt Church.

In an elevated position on the north wall outside Stanton Harcourt Church is a sad memorial to two young lovers who died in each other's arms; struck by lightning. It was an event witnessed by Alexander Pope, who was so moved by the incident as to relate it in several letters to friends. In a letter to Lady Mary Wortley Montagu, he describes the event in detail.

'I have just passed part of this summer in an old romantic seat of my Lord Harcourt which he lent to me. It overlooks a common-field where under the shade of a haycock, sat two lovers, as constant as ever were found in romance, beneath a spreading beech. The name of the one (let it sound as it will) was John Hewet; and the other Sarah Drew. John was a well-set man about five and twenty, Sarah a brown woman of eighteen . . . Their love was the talk, but not the scandal of the whole neighbourhood; for all they aimed at was the blameless possession of each other in marriage. It was but this very morning that he had obtained her parents' consent, and it was but until the next week that they were to wait to be happy . . . While they were employed (it was on the last of July) a terrible storm of thunder and lightning arose, that drove the labourers to what shelter the trees and hedges afforded. Sarah, frighted and out of breath, sunk on a haycock, and John (who never separated from her) sat by her side, having raked two or three heaps together to secure her. Immediately, there was so loud a crack as if Heaven had burst asunder. The labourers, all solicitous for each others safety called to one another: those that were nearest to our lovers, hearing no answer stepped to the place where they lay: they first saw a little smoke, and after, this faithful pair;

John with one arm about his Sarah's neck and the other held over her face as if to screen her from the lighning. They were struck dead.'

The sweethearts were buried together in the churchyard. At Pope's request, a memorial stone for which he wrote the epitaph, was placed on the grave.

FARINGDON

'AFRICA' IN FARINGDON

Location: Faringdon House.

Access: Though Faringdon House is privately owned the park is opened to the public on Easter Mondays at the owner's discretion.

Leaving Faringdon on the A4095 road to Witney, you pass beneath the long stone wall of Faringdon House. Because the wall is on the nearside, you could easily miss the rather incongruous stone statue that stands in the park just over the wall. It is one of two, brought to Faringdon by Mr.Robert Heber Percy in the 1960s from the gardens of Crystal Palace, where it had been since the Great Exhibition of 1851. Its companion, sited further into the park, represents 'Asia', and the statue you see from the road depicts the shrouded figure of 'Africa', leaning on what appears to be the head of the Sphinx. The statue of 'Africa' was set on its present site to hide an ugly concrete machine gun post left over from World War II. There is an interesting mural depicting both statues, in Faringdon's Bell Hotel.

Africa.

Asia.

FARINGDON

LORD BERNER'S FOLLY

Location:	A half mile east of Faringdon.
Access:	Only occasional public access to tower.

Faringdon Folly was built by Lord Berner, a retired diplomat who was inclined to practical jokes. He declared: 'The great point of the tower is that it will be entirely useless. I want to stand on top of it and look around me'. In fact that was not quite the case, for it was built during the 1930s depression, and provided valuable work for the unemployed; so it was not quite as useless as his Lordship made out. He did, however, think there could be some who might consider it a useful way of leaving the problems of this world behind, so he erected a notice saying: 'Members of the public committing suicide from this tower do so at their own risk.' It is built of red brick and stands 140 feet high, on a hill, east of the town.

There were numerous objectors to its construction. One, a retired Admiral, complained that the tower would obstruct the view from his house. Lord Berner's lawyers pointed out that the tower could only be seen from the Admiral's house if he used a telescope. The Admiral countered with the salty remark: 'Of course it was only visible through a telescope; how else would you expect an Admiral to view the scenery?'

Its opening on November 5th 1935, was celebrated with a grand fireworks display.

GREAT COXWELL

THE GREATEST MEDIEVAL TITHE BARN IN ENGLAND!

Location:	Great Coxwell, Faringdon.
Access:	Open daily – National Trust.

In 1204, King John gave the Manor of Faringdon to the Cistercian Abbey of Beaulieu in Hampshire. The monks established a cell at Great Coxwell, and the Great Tithe Barn we see today was probably completed later in the century. The barn was controlled by the monks of Beaulieu until Henry VIII dissolved the monasteries, after which it passed into the ownership of the Mores family. Little of its history is recorded until the 18th century, when it became the property of the Pleydell-Bouverie family. In 1956, it was bought by Mr. E .E. Cook who bequeathed it to the National Trust.

Built of Cotswold stone, the barn is 152ft long, 44ft wide and 48ft high at the ridge. The roof of graded courses of Cotswold stone tiles, is supported inside by two rows of oak posts standing on 7ft high stone plinths. These same posts have held up this roof for the 700 years since its construction. In his book *The Barns of the Abbey of Beaulieu at its Granges of Great Coxwell & Beaulieu St. Leonards,* Professor Walter Horn has described the Great Barn at Coxwell as 'the finest of the surviving medieval barns in England, and one of the most impressive structures of its kind in Europe.'

LECHLADE

OLD FATHER THAMES

Location: St. John's Lock.

Access: Open to the public.

Take the A417 from
Lechlade to Faringdon;
after a mile you pass
The Trout on left
where you cross the
river bridge and park
immediately on right.

High in the hills,
Down in the dales
Happy and fancy free.
Old Father Thames
Keeps rolling along
Down to the mighty
sea.

Though Lechlade is in Gloucestershire, St. John's Lock is on the Oxfordshire side of the River Thames which separates these two glorious counties. The three-ton bearded figure of Old Father Thames reclines on the side of the lock. By his side is a barrel and several bundles tied with rope. They presumably represent the cargo brought to the Thames by ships from all over the world. There is also a shield which seems to bear the City of London Coat of Arms.

Like the statues of 'Africa' and 'Asia' at Faringdon House, Father Thames was originally sited at Crystal Palace in London for the Great Exhibition. They were all sold off some years ago by London County Council, Father Thames being bought for the garden the Hon. Michael Berry, son of Lord Camrose. In 1957, Mr. H. Scott Freeman, Conservator of the Thames Conservancy Board, purchased the statue to commemorate the Board's centenary. It was placed at Thames Head in Trewsbury Mead, 3 1/2 miles south-west of Cirencester, which is now accepted as the source of the river, though this has not always been so. Seven Springs near Coberley, south of Cheltenham also claims the distinction, but this was officially discounted in 1937. The statue would have stayed at Thames Head, but in latter years vandalism caused its removal to the safety of St. John's Lock.

KELMSCOTT

KELMSCOTT MANOR – HOME OF WILLIAM MORRIS AND THE PRE-RAPHAELITES

Location:	Leave Lechlade on A417 Faringdon road proceed two miles and turn left to Kelmscott just before 'The Trout'. Signposted from here.
Access:	Open to the public every Wednesday from April-September 11am-1pm & 2pm-5pm. Refreshments available.

Kelmscott Manor is set on the banks of the upper Thames which glides silently through the garden. The original gable-fronted house of Cotswold stone, was built in 1570, and extended in later years. It was here that the artist, writer and socialist William Morris made his home from 1871. Though he and his family occupied Kelmscott Manor until his death in 1896, he never owned the house. With fellow Pre-Raphaelite Dante Gabriel Rossetti, Morris held a joint tenancy of the manor where they lived together until Rossetti's departure in 1874. Here, Rossetti was inspired to write poetry and pursue his life as an artist, frequently using Morris's wife Jane as a model, as Morris himself had done. Although they had two daughters, Morris's marriage was a disaster, and it was no surprise that Jane fell under the spell of Rossetti with whom she had a prolonged affair.

There are many examples of Morris's fabric and wallpaper designs in the house, as well as Jane's embroidery. Of Rossetti's work, there are numerous sensitive drawings and paintings of Morris's wife and children. Though the house is not furnished quite as it was when the family lived there, there is still a good deal of their furniture and personal belongings. Morris's greatcoat hangs on the back of a door, ready to be donned for a brisk autumn walk. In his bedroom is the solid oak four-poster bed in which he was born, with colourful hangings, and a valance on which his wife and daughter May exquisitely embroidered his poem 'For the Bed at Kelmscott', written in 1891.

> *The Wind's on the wold and the night is a-cold*
> *And Thames runs chill twixt mead and hill*
> *But kind and dear is the old house here.*

Kelmscott Manor is not a stagnant museum of a bygone age, but a creditable manifestation of William Morris and his Pre-Raphaelite friends. He died in 1896, and is buried with his wife in Kelmscott village churchyard. On the 'Memorial Cottages' in the village, there is a carved plaque of Morris musing in the Home Mead at Kelmscott.

East Front, Kelmscott Manor.

'William Morris muses in his garden'. Carving by George Jack on the Memorial Cottages in Kelmscott village.

BURFORD

ANTHONY SEDLEY 1649 – PRISNER & A MEMORIAL TO PRISONERS
EXECUTED BY CROMWELL

Location:	Burford Parish Church.
Access:	Open during normal church hours.

There would seem little particularly odd about a Norman font in an English country church, but a crudely scored inscription on the lead lining of the font in Burford parish church makes it an object of particular curiosity. The inscription reads ANTHONY SEDLEY 1649 – PRISNER. Who was Sedley, and why was he a prisoner? He was one of

that band of men known as The Levellers; disgruntled troops in Oliver Cromwell's army. On May Day 1649, a large number of them broke away from the main troop at Salisbury, and set off for Banbury. Marching by way of Marlborough and Wantage, they arrived at Burford on the 13th May, and there bedded down for the night. While they were sleeping, they were surprised by Cromwell's men who took 340 prisoners. It was while they awaited their fate under guard in the church that Anthony Sedley wrote his name into the pages of history by scoring a message on the font that has survived to this day. On the 17th May, the prisoners were taken onto the roof of the church to witness the execution of their ringleaders, Cornet Thompson, Corporal Perkins and Corporal Church, who were put against a wall and shot. The three were buried in unmarked graves, and only a simple plaque on the outside wall of the Lady Chapel records their suffering.

BURFORD

HERCULES HASTINGS' TURRET CLOCK

Location: Burford Parish Church.

The earliest mention of a church clock in Burford seems to have been in the Church Wardens' Accounts of 1625. The church bells were mentioned in 1626. Through these Accounts, the history of the church clock and chimes can be traced for the next 300 years. In 1670, Mr. Yonge of Oxford was paid the monumental sum of £16.00 for '. . . the chime and all other materials belonging to it.' In the same year, 3s/0d was paid for a 'waite for the chime.' and 12s/0d to Mr. Yate, 'for fitching the chime from Oxford.' The clock, it seems, consumed a prodigious amount of oil '. . . 2s/6d for oyle for clock, bells and chimes att sevrall times.'

In 1685 a new Turret Clock was installed by Hercules Hastings of Burford, for which he was paid the princely sum of £10.00. According to the Church Wardens' Accounts, the new turret clock mechanism drove the hands of the clock on the side of the church tower. A long pendulum hung through the floor in the tower, probably similar to the one that can still be seen working in the church at Garsington.

Hastings' mechanism powered the clock for over 300 years, until its replacement in 1940. Though many of its parts were replaced during its working life, the frame now to be seen in the north transept is original.

BURFORD

THE TANFIELD TOMB

> *Location:* Burford Parish Church.

Sir Lawrence Tanfield, Lord Chief Baron of the Exchequer at the Court of James I, died at 2am on 30th April 1625. The parish register records that he 'was buried the first day of May at 12 of the clock in the night.' The haste of his burial was not altogether unusual, and might have been due to the fear of smallpox. The magnificent edifice we see in the church today was erected by his grieving widow. She planned for it to be placed in Westminster Abbey; but it was not to be, for she died shortly after, and joined her husband in the tomb. Lady Tanfield was deeply unpopular in Burford, and local folk believed that when she died, her spirit flew over the town in a burning chariot. Burford's simple townsfolk begged the vicar to rid them of her spirit, and he responded by trapping it in a bottle, which he threw into the river Windrush.

In contrast to the grand effigies of Sir Lawrence & Lady Tanfield lying on top of the tomb is the chilling sight of the skeleton lying underneath. Their daughter Elizabeth kneels at their head, and at their feet, their grandson Lucius Cary, 2nd Lord Falkland, who died at the battle of Newbury.

There is so much of curious interest in Burford Parish Church; more than could be included here. But look out for the tomb of Edmund Harman, Barber and Courtier to Henry VIII. Also, the sad little weeping cherub on Christopher Kempster's memorial, and the mysterious stone that marks the burial place of the murdered – John Pryor – Gent, whose body was found hidden in the priory garden on 3rd April 1697. A real historical 'who dun it?'

Sir Lawrence and Lady Tanfield's tomb, Burford Parish Church.

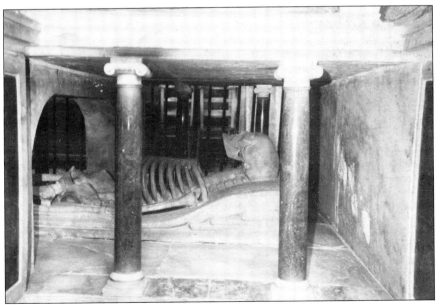

Cadaver beneath the Tanfield tomb, Burford Parish Church.

SWINBROOK

THE FETTIPLACE TOMBS

> *Location:* Swinbrook Village Church, 3 miles east of Burford.

It is unlikely that motorists racing along the busy main road from Oxford to Cheltenham, will notice the signpost to Swinbrook. Even fewer will venture off the A40 'race track' to explore the peaceful haven that lies a mile or so down the quiet country lane. Set on the banks of the tranquil Windrush, the lovely village of Swinbrook has one of the most interesting churches in Oxfordshire. Its misericords are fascinating, as are the stained-glass windows that record for posterity, a German landmine that dropped in a field during the second world war, damaging the church and several cottages nearby.

But perhaps the most curious objects in this 12th century church are the magnificent Fettiplace monuments. They consist of six marble effigies in two triple tiers, reclining in a seemingly casual way, one above the other. The first tier in Tudor style, outside the sanctuary was ordered by the first Sir Edmund Fettiplace, for his grandfather, his father and himself. He died in 1613. The second tier in Stuart style, inside the sanctuary was ordered by the second Sir Edmund Fettiplace, for his uncle, his father and himself. He died in 1686. The Fettiplace family ranked among the wealthiest landowners in the county, and a timeless jingle reminds us of their wealth.

> *The Tracys, the Lacys and the Fettiplaces,*
> *Own all the woods, the parks and places.*

For over four hundred years, they lived in Swinbrook House, said to have been the finest Tudor manor in the county. Sadly, nothing now remains of either the manor or the family.

Outside, near to the church porch, are the two simple gravestones of the Mitford sisters, Unity and Nancy.

*The Second
World War
land-mine
memorial
window.*

The Fettiplace tombs, Swinbrook Church.

MINSTER LOVELL

WHO LIES IN THIS MYSTERIOUS TOMB?

> *Location:* St. Kennelm Church.

The main, north door of St. Kennelm Church is known as the christening door. It is opposite the devil's door, which is always left open to let the devil out and evil spirits escape when a baby cries at the touch of holy water.

As you enter the church, your eyes are immediately drawn to an ornate alabaster tomb, embellished with ten colourful shields of arms. Reclining on top in an attitude of prayer is the figure of a 15th century knight in armour, but as the tomb bears no inscription to say who lies within, its occupant has long been the subject of speculation.

It is almost certainly a Lovel, and there are some clues to suggest which one it might be. The favourite seems to be William 7th Baron, who died in 1455. Forced by ill health to return to England from France following the execution of Joan of Arc in 1431, he chose to live by the Windrush at Minster Lovell. Here he demolished the 12th century house and church, and in their place, built a modern manor and a church which he dedicated to Cotswold Saint Kennelm. The shields of arms on the tomb provide a clue, as does the beautifully-sculptured figure of St. Christopher on the tomb's west end. William had a special attachment to the Saint, having founded the Guild of Saint Christopher, with his brother-in-law Lord Cromwell, Lord Sudeley and Richard Quartermain. But the experts are still not completely convinced; so the occupant of the alabaster tomb remains a mystery. But if Lord Lovel does not lie in the tomb, who does?

MINSTER LOVELL

MINSTER LOVELL HALL – LORD FRANCIS LOVEL AND THE SKELETON MYSTERY

:

Access: Open daily, Easter to October 2pm-5pm – English Heritage.

The ruins of Minster Lovell Hall are all that remain of the magnificent manor built by William Lovel between 1431 and 1442. On his death in 1455, William was succeeded by John, his son, who was succeeded in 1468 by Francis, most powerful of all the Lovels.

> *'The catte, the ratte, and Lovel our dogge*
> *Rule all England under the hogge'.*

This historic rhyme reflects the influence of Francis Lovel, 'our dogge', who with Sir William Catesby, 'the catte', and Sir Richard Ratcliffe, 'the ratte' were the three most powerful men in England, during the reign of the Yorkist Richard III, known as 'the hogge' for the boar on his coat of arms.

Created a Viscount in 1483, Francis fought for his king in the Wars of the Roses. He was at the Battle of Bosworth in 1485, when Richard was killed fighting Henry Tudor. Escapintg to Flanders, he later returned to challenge the Lancastrian King Henry in Simnel's rebellion. After fighting at the Battle of Stoke, he was variously reported killed in action, drowned in the river Trent, and escaped to the continent. He might have disappeared without trace were it not for the mystery that surrounds his fate. Some gossip says that having survived the Battle of Stoke, he went back home to Minster Lovell. But now with a price on his head, there were few he could trust. It is said he hid in an underground vault known only to one of his servants who fed him each day, and kept his door securely locked. Some say the servant died very suddenly; but others who know, say he turned against his master. Whatever the reason, poor Francis was helplessly trapped in his secret cell, for nobody knew he was there. Nothing was heard of him until William Cowper, the Clerk of Parliament related that in 1728, the Duke of Rutland told him how some twenty years earlier, workmen laying a

drain discovered a large underground vault in which there was the entire skeleton of a man. It was sitting at a table with a book, some paper and a pen. A decaying cap lay nearby, and on this evidence, the family and others concluded it was the missing Lord Francis.

MINSTER LOVELL

MEDIEVAL MANORIAL DOVECOTE

Location:	Minster Lovell Manor.
Access:	Open daily, Easter to October 2pm-5pm – English Heritage. Follow the path skirting the land and building on the riverside.

When in 1431, William Lovel returned from the French wars, he decided to settle in Minster Lovell where he built a new manor. It was regarded as one of the finest manor houses in Oxfordshire, and like many such houses, it had a dovecote. Unlike the house, the dovecote has survived and stands today in perfect condition, thanks to careful restoration by English Heritage. Built of Cotswold stone, it is circular shaped with a conical roof and a central hole for pigeons to enter. The pigeons nested in small tiered recesses round the inside walls, where young birds known as squabs were reared for the manorial table.

Public access to such buildings is not normally permitted, but here visitors may go inside and see the elaborate structure of timbers that make up the roof. It is an excellent example of medieval craftsmanship and well worth visitors' attention.

Interior of Medieval Dovecote.

WITNEY

THE OLD BLANKET HALL

Location: High Street.

Not so very long ago, you could mention the name of a town or a county and immediately identify it with a product that sustained a whole community. Lancashire cotton, South Wales coal, Northamptonshire footwear. But the face of Britain is rapidly changing; most of Lancashire's cotton mills have closed, and coal mining in Wales is almost extinct. Yet in spite of all the changes, the name of the Cotswold market town of Witney is still synonymous with blankets and wool. Blankets have been made in Witney since the Middle Ages. In 1279, local records mention Edmund the Fuller, Elias Weaver and Geoffrey Dyer; proof, if proof were needed, of its long association with the products of wool. The weavers formed a Guild in 1711, and were granted a Charter by Queen Anne. Wool has served Witney well; at the height of its prosperity there were five mills in the area. Now there is only one; Early's Witney Mill; still the best-known name in blanket making.

In 1721, the weavers built the Blanket Hall on Witney High Street. It had a faceless clock with a bell to strike the hours. A face was later added, with only one hand to tell the quarter hours, but not the minutes. Beneath the clock is the Blanket Makers' coat of arms. Every blanket made in and around Witney was brought to the hall to be measured and weighed before it was given the mark of approval.

WITNEY

THE BUTTERCROSS

Location: Market Place.

The Buttercross stands in the Market Place at the very heart of Witney. Here sheep were bought and sold until the 1950s. Its central pillar was probably the base of an old preaching cross. In 1606, Richard Ashcombe gave £50 to build a cover for the cross, and in 1683, a bequest by William Blake of Cogges provided money for a clock and a sundial to be placed on top. Opposite the Buttercross is the 17th century Town Hall. Under its arches, grain was bought and sold until the Corn Exchange was built in the 17th century.

SHIPTON UNDER WYCHWOOD

A MEMORIAL TO FOUR TRAGIC EMIGRANT FAMILIES

Location: Village Green.

On the village green, close to a 15th century inn bearing the intriguing name of The Shaven Crown, an obelisk stands as a tragic memorial to seventeen parishioners. They were members of four families who set out to emigrate to New Zealand in 1874. The ship on which they were travelling caught fire off Tristan da Cunah, and with 470 fellow passengers, the Shipton emigrants perished.

All are remembered on this sad memorial. Henry Townsend, 62; his wife Ann, 53; Jane Townsend, 35, and two children; her husband George Charter, 31; Henry Hedges, 30; Mary Townsend, his wife, and their three children; Richard Hedges, 56, and Sarah, his wife, 53; Charles Hedges, 18, son of Richard and Sarah; John Hedges, 24, and Sarah, his wife, 22; Thomas Hedges, 27.

In 1974, a tree was planted to mark the centenary of the tragedy.

CHURCHILL

IN MEMORY OF WILLIAM SMITH – FATHER OF BRITISH GEOLOGY

Location:	Churchill Village.

William Smith came from farming stock and was the eldest of four children. Born at Churchill in 1769, he went to the village school. Solitary and studious as a child, he collected fossils on long lonely walks in the fields around Churchill. On leaving school, he went to work for Edward Webb, a surveyor at Stow-on-the-Wold, where he learnt about the soil and the underlying rocks in Oxfordshire and adjacent counties. England was on the threshold of the Industrial Revolution, and Smith was widely engaged in canal and mining excavation. He was an expert in drainage and irrigation, and in 1810 when failure of the hot springs threatened the prosperity of Bath Spa, he located the leak and found a new channel, so the waters flowed more freely than before.

In 1819 he started work on his New Geological Atlas Of England & Wales, which was published in six parts. It was an expensive undertaking that nearly brought about his financial ruin. Threatened with bankruptcy, he was forced to sell almost all he possessed; his home, books and even his drawings. Only the kindness of a friend saved him from total disaster. His Atlas did, however, establish him as the 'father of British geology', and in 1831, the Council of the Geological Society awarded him the Wollaston Medal at a meeting in Oxford. He died in 1839 at Northampton, and is buried in St.Peter's Church where there is a memorial tablet and a bust.

CHURCHILL

ANOTHER 'MAGDALEN' TOWER?

Location: All Saints' Church.

Access: Can be viewed from outside.

There can be little doubt that the most striking object of interest in the village of Churchill is the church tower. But this is no ordinary tower as you will see on closer inspection. To anyone who knows Oxford, and particularly Magdalen College, the tower will have a familiar look. Compare it with the picture of Magdalen Tower, and you will see that the two are almost identical. The tower at Churchill was designed by Oxfordshire architect James Plowman who produced a replica of Magdalen College Tower, two thirds the size of the original. He also used the roof of Christchurch Hall as his model for the hammer beam roof of the church, and buttresses similar to those of New College Chapel.

JUNIPER HILL, COTTISFORD & FRINGFORD

FLORA THOMPSON'S 'LARK RISE', 'FORDLOW' & 'CANDLEFORD GREEN'

> *Location:* Juniper Hill (Lark Rise) lies just off the A43, 19 miles north of
> Oxford. Fringford (Candleford Green) is off the A421 Bicester to
> Buckingham road. Cottisford (Fordlow) is about 2 miles north of
> Fringford.

You will have to look hard for Juniper Hill on the map. A scattering of cottages
built for the poor of Cottisford, it is the tiny hamlet where Flora Thompson was
born in 1876. Her enchanting trilogy, *Lark Rise to Candleford*, is a national
treasure. It is a sensitive autobiographical tale of rural life in late-Victorian
Oxfordshire; an era long since past, when village life flourished. A time when the
inn, the church and school knitted the scattered cottage dwellers into a village
community. Each day, from the age of five, until she was twelve, Flora walked
from Juniper Hill, her 'Lark Rise', to school in the 'mother village' of Cottisford,
the 'Fordlow' of her book, a mile and a half away.

Flora lived with her mother and father, and brothers and sisters, in a small
thatched cottage at Juniper Hill. In *Lark Rise to Candleford*, she describes it as
'. . . a small grey stone cottage with a thatched roof, a green-painted door, and a
plum tree trained up the wall to the eaves.' Known as the end house, it stood a
little apart from the others, seeming, she says, to turn its back on the neighbours.
'All around from every quarter, the stiff clayey soil of the arable fields crept up;
bare brown and windswept for eight months out of the twelve. Spring brought a
flush of green wheat and there were violets under the hedges, and pussy willow
out by the brook at the bottom of Hundred Acres; but only for a few weeks in
late summer, had the landscape real beauty. Then the ripened cornfields rippled
up to the doorsteps of the cottages and the hamlet became an island in a sea of
dark gold.'

Lovers of 'Lark Rise' can still enjoy that scene today, and the larks that gave her
hamlet its name, still sing in the heavens high above Juniper Hill. A few miles
distant is the village of Fringford, to which Flora gave the name 'Candleford
Green'. It was here she took her first job in the Post Office, adjacent to the
village blacksmith's forge. Though the Post Office and forge are long since gone,
the old thatched building that housed them is little changed in appearance from
what it was in Flora's day.

The Cottage at Juniper Hill has changed little since Flora lived there as a child. Notice the plaque on the right, close to the top window.

'Candleford Green', Fringford. The Old Post Office and Blacksmith's Forge, now a private house, is little changed since Flora's days.

STOKE LYNE

AN OBELISK FOR A FAVOURITE FOXHOUND

Location:	In a field at the rear of Bainton Farmhouse in the hamlet of Bainton. Take A421 Buckingham road from Bicester; turn left for Stoke Lyne and left again at the Bainton sign.
Access:	Visitors are reminded that the field is private property and part of a working farm, You are urged to take great care, particularly if there are crops in the field.

Erected in 1812
By Sir Thomas Mostyn Bart. M.P.
M.F.H. Bicester Hounds 1800 to 1830
In Memory Of His Favourite Hound
'LADY'.

This brief inscription on an obelisk in a field at Bainton, not far from Juniper Hill, prompts one to ask – Why a memorial to a foxhound?

The obelisk tells us little. To find the answer you would have to travel two hundred miles north west of Oxford, to Beaumaris on the Isle of Anglesey, where another memorial on Lady's grave bears the following inscription.

> *Of all the Ladies live or dead,*
> *In the chase that we have sped,*
> *Here the honoured relics rest,*
> *Of the fleetest and the best.*
> *From the best the best are bred*
> *And in truth it may be said,*
> *Lady if we hope to see,*
> *A better Lady, 'tis from thee.*

Huntsmen get very attached to their hounds, and usually have a particular favourite. 'Lady' was the favourite hound of Sir Thomas Mostyn, who was Master of the Bicester Foxhounds for almost thirty years. He also had a pack of hounds on his estate at Mostyn in North Wales.

One day, the Mostyn Hounds were hunting over the border in Shropshire. 'Lady' was heavily in whelp, and should really have stayed back at kennels, but somehow she managed to get in with the pack. Out hunting, she decided her puppies were due, and alone made her way back to the kennels at Mostyn. It was an astonishing feat, for she covered a distance of at least fifty miles. As usual, she produced a litter of superb puppies of the highest hunting quality.

Hound enthusiasts might be interested to know that 'Lady' was born in 1801, and died in 1812. Her sire was a hound called 'Grasper' out of a bitch called 'Whimsey'. Both hounds belonged to Sir William Lowther.

'Lady' with her puppies. (Courtesy of 'Hounds' Magazine)

SPELSBURY

HERE LIE THE FOREBEARS OF ROBERT E. LEE

Location: All Saints Church, Spelsbury.

The vaults in Spelsbury Church are filled with the mortal remains of the Lee family whose splendid marble memorials adorn the chancel. Most interesting is the tomb of Sir Henry Lee who married the daughter of Charles II and Lady Castlemaine when he and his bride were only 15 and 13 years old. In spite of marrying so young, they were happily married for 40 years during which time they produced 18 children. American visitors will be interested to know that Sir Henry was an ancestor of their own famous General Robert E. Lee.

Nearby, a brass plate set in the floor of the nave is a less splendid though no less enduring memorial to George Pickering, an old Lee family servant. Even in death, he was expected to know his place and not get too close to 'his great masters'. The poignant inscription reads:

> *'George Pickering Gentleman having been thirty years a servant of the honorouble family of the Lees of Ditchly about the LXX1 Yeare of his age the X111 day of March Anno Domini 1645 departed this life and lyeth here buried not to prophane (by a rude touch) the dust of his great masters doe we bouldly thrust this aged servants bones whose humble love and innocent ambition did move by creeping neere their tombes adored side to show his body not his duty dyde.'*

There is an interesting collection of brass nameplates on the north wall of the church, taken from the Lee family coffins.

CHIPPING NORTON

AN UNUSUAL MEMORIAL TO A LOVER OF HORSES

Location:	Chipping Norton Cemetery.
Access:	100 yards along the path on the left, just past the lodge.

There can be few memorials as unusual as the black marble five-barred gate that marks the grave of Davy Barnard. An ordinary sort of chap, Davy was well known and respected for his knowledge and love of horses; they were his life. He owned, raced and showed them all over the country, and even had one trained at Newmarket. No lesser enthusiast was his wife Daisy. She shared her husband's interest and her poignant epitaph tells its own story. When Davy died in 1973, at the early age of 48, there could only be one fitting memorial; a five-barred gate with a horse's head framed in a horseshoe.

CHIPPING NORTON

BLISS MILL – A HISTORY OF COTSWOLD WOOL

Location: On A44 Chipping Norton – Moreton in Marsh road.

Industry? In the heart of rural England? Somewhat incongruous you might think, until you learn that for generations, Bliss Mill produced high quality tweeds from Cotswold wool. It was a time when the Cotswolds prospered on wool from local sheep known as 'Cotswold Lions.'

The founder of the Bliss tradition in Chipping Norton was a young man from Chalford, in the Stroud Valley, whose family had been in wool for nigh on three hundred years. In 1756 young Thomas Bliss crossed the hills from Stroud to sell his father's cloth in Chipping Norton. He stayed at the Swan Inn, where he fell in love with Ann, the landlord's daughter. They married and he would have taken her back to Chalford, but as she wouldn't leave home they settled in Chipping Norton.

Her father bought them a small cottage cloth-making business to give them a start in life. Of their ten children, the fourth son, William, followed his father into cloth making but for some strange reason, the firm became known as William Bliss & Sisters. He made a strong cloth called 'kersey checks'. Demand was so great, that in 1804 production moved to Lower Mill, a new factory converted from an old malthouse.

William married Hanna Lay on Christmas Eve in 1792. They had nine children. Their son William, born in 1810, took over the business in 1839, and under him it went from strength to strength. In 1855 he rebuilt Lower Mill, enlarging it in 1865, when steam was used to power some of the finest machinery in the land. In 1872, a fire completely gutted the mill in less than three hours. It was a catastrophe for the family and for the town.

Within a year, a new mill rose from the ashes, considered '. . . the best built and most ornamental mill in the three kingdoms'. To celebrate the opening, over 900 men, women and children sat down to high tea. But the disaster proved too much for the family's finances, and after William's death in 1884, his only son, another William, was forced to form a limited company. He left for New Zealand in 1896, but the business he left behind continued to prosper under its new owners, Fox Bros., of Wellington. The mill was closed when production was transferred to Somerset in 1980.

Now a protected building with all its fine architectural features preserved, the mill looks magnificent as ever. Its recent conversion to luxury apartments has given it a new lease of life.

Bliss Mill, Chipping Norton.

CHIPPING NORTON

THE THEATRE THAT WAS ONCE A CITADEL

Location:	Spring Street, Chipping Norton.
Access:	Telephone: (Admin) 01608-642349 or (Box Office) 01608-642350.

Viewed from a distance, The Theatre at Chipping Norton does not look out of the ordinary. But take a closer look, and you will see some rather unusual plaques set in its walls. The plaques are a clue to the building's origin, for what now houses The Theatre, started life in 1888, as a Salvation Army Citadel. By all accounts, the people of Chipping Norton are better disposed to The Theatre than they were to the arrival in the town of the Salvation Army. According to a report in the 'War Cry' of April 1888, a gang known as The Skeleton Army, attacked the Salvationist 'Soldiers' on the way to their meetings. But hostility and violence were nothing new to the Salvation Army which characteristically went on the attack with the declaration: 'We have opened fire on this town in right good earnest. The work of God has gone on in a most marvellous manner in spite of every foe.' The Salvationists won, and in August, Commandant Herbert Booth and his lieutenants laid the foundation stones. These are the stones to be seen at the front of The Theatre and in the auditorium to commemorate their early struggles; one reads:

> *'These stones were laid by one hundred of those who through great persecution boldly and conscientiously served their God.'*

When the Salvation Army moved out in the 1960s, the Citadel was reduced to the undignified role of a furniture warehouse. But the doors of a building designed and constructed by men who built the old Victorian Music Halls, can't stay closed to the public for long. In 1968, John and Tamara Malcolm of the Royal Shakespeare Company, saw the building's potential, and set about transforming it into The Theatre we see today. Money to finance their ambitious undertaking was raised through Public Appeals. With the help of enthusiasts and well-wishers the new, extended Theatre was opened with a Gala Evening in 1993. Donations are still urgently needed and can be sent direct to The Theatre at Chipping Norton.

MORETON IN MARSH

THE FOUR SHIRES STONE

Location: On A44, 2 miles east of Moreton in Marsh at Gt. Wolford turn.

The Four Shires Stone is a large sculptured pillar of Cotswold stone standing just off the A44 at the turn for Great Wolford. On each of the stone's four sides is inscribed the name of one of the counties – Oxfordshire, Gloucestershire, Warwickshire and Worcestershire which come together not far from here.

GREAT ROLLRIGHT

THE MYSTERIOUS ROLLRIGHT STONES

> *Location:*   Between A34 & A44, north-west of Chipping Norton.

The Rollright Stones are steeped in myth and legend. They are thought to pre-date 1500 B.C., and are considered almost equal in importance to Stonehenge and Avebury. There are three groups of stones, on each side of the road connecting the A34 and A44, north-west of Chipping Norton. The larger group, known as the King's Men, forms a circle of 77 roughly-hewn stones, though legend says they cannot be counted. Perhaps most interesting is the solitary King Stone. Tall, majestic, and somewhat mysterious, it stands alone on a mound as befits an ancient King. Some 300 yards distant in a field opposite, are the Whispering Knights; a group of four upright stones, with a fifth prostrated. It is thought they formed part of the chamber in a burial mound, of which there is now no trace.

According to legend, a nameless king who set out to conquer England, climbed Rollright Hill with his army. He was stopped by a witch who told him that if, after seven strides, he could see Long Compton, he would be King of England. He took seven strides, but a mound rose up before him and obscured the view, whereupon the King and his men were turned to stones by the witch, who turned herself into an elder tree. Witches had a reputation for turning themselves into elders, and an elder tree still stood between the King and his men until the 18th century.

The King's Men.

The King.

The Whispering Knights.

CHURCH ENSTONE

STEVENS WISDOM PRAYING AT HIS OWN TOMBSTONE

Location: St. Kennelm's Church, Church Enstone.

In the quiet backwater of Church Enstone is the mellow Cotswold stone church of St. Kennelm. Of particular interest in the south aisle of this lovely church is the rather odd tomb of Stevens Wisdom. It consists of a colourful statue of Stevens kneeling in prayer in front of his own gravestone, which is curiously inscribed with the date of his death in 1633.

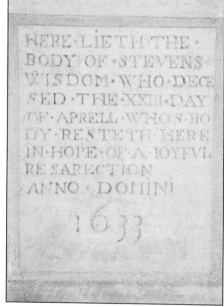

CHASTLETON

CHASTLETON HOUSE – A JACOBEAN TREASURE

Location:	Off A44, 4 miles north west of Chipping Norton.
Access:	The National Trust is planning to open the house to the public late in 1996 or early 1997.

Chastleton House is a national treasure. This perfect example of a Jacobean manor was built by Walter Jones, a 'new man' and lawyer who acquired the manor and village of Chastleton in 1605. The family occupied the house continuously until 1991. Unspoiled and almost unchanged from the time it was built, it retains much of its original furnishings including some that appeared in the inventory of 1633. Its design is attributed to Robert Smythson, architect of Longleat and Hardwick Hall. The south front is regarded

as one of the most unusual and sophisticated compositions of English Renaissance architecture.

Inside, the long gallery runs the whole length of an upper floor, affording magnificent views, from the windows. The church to the side of the house dates from the 12th century, and an interesting stone dovecote stands in a field to the front.

Chastleton House has witnessed many historic events. It was once owned by Robert Catesby, one of the conspirators in Guy Fawke's Gun Powder Plot to blow up Parliament. During the Civil War, Arthur Jones, an ardent Royalist, was pursued from Worcester by Cromwell's men who thought he was the escaping Prince Charles.

Since it was built almost four centuries ago, the house has suffered from a lack of money to provide adequate maintenance. Some consider this to have been a mixed blessing, since it restrained the hands of would-be restorers. Thankfully, Chastleton has found a friend in the National Trust who rescued it in 1991, and immediately embarked on a multi-million pound programme of conservation. The Trust is committed to conservation rather than restoration, to preserve the fabric of the building and its contents and retain its romantic atmosphere.

MILCOMBE

18TH CENTURY DOVECOTE

Location:	Manor Farm, Milcombe, 1½ miles south west of Bloxham.
Access:	Can be viewed from outside.

From 1563 to 1625, the Dalby family occupied Milcombe Hall, which was remodelled in the early 18th century by Sir John Thorneycroft. Sadly, little now remains of Milcombe Hall, which was almost entirely demolished in 1953. What was left was converted into a small farmhouse in 1964. Now known as Manor Farm, it retained the 19th century Gothic front and original mullioned windows. Above a blocked-up doorway is the date 1630. Happily the 18th century octagonal stone dovecote survived. Standing apart from the farmhouse, its elegant structure easily attracts the attention of the casual passer-by. It has four dormer windows on an octagonal stone tiled roof, which is crowned by an open cupola.

There are plans to renovate the dovecote and build houses in fairly close proximity. But it seems that sensitive planning has allowed for an area of lawn to surround it, and who knows, they might even persuade the doves to come back!

BANBURY

RIDE A COCK HORSE TO BANBURY CROSS

Location: Town Centre.

For most people, the mention of Banbury Cross evokes memories of childhood, and the nursery rhyme:

Ride a cock horse to Banbury Cross,
To see a fine lady upon a white horse;
With rings on her fingers and bells on her toes;
She shall have music wherever she goes.

The rhyme is known to be centuries old, and there are several recorded variations. There were three crosses in various parts of Banbury in the Middle Ages. A White Cross, a Market Cross and a High or Bread Cross in Butchers Row. In the 16th century, the town gained a reputation for Puritanism. But the Puritans disliked the crosses which they condemned as pagan. By 1621, all three had either been destroyed or mutilated.

In 1858, the wedding of Queen Victoria's eldest daughter gave the people of Banbury an opportunity to erect a new cross at its centre, and this is the cross we see today. It is a finely carved stone monument standing 52ft 6ins high. The statues of Queen Victoria, King Edward VII and King George V were added to celebrate the coronation of George V in 1911.

WROXTON

AN UNCOMMON THATCHED CATHOLIC CHAPEL

Location: On the A422 Banbury to Stratford road.

Wroxton's tiny Roman Catholic chapel is rather unusual. Standing beside the busy A422 Banbury to Stratford road, it is one of a very few English churches with a thatched roof. Though it bears the name of the martyred St. Thomas of Canterbury, it does not have the grand historic associations or the tranquil situation of the village church nearby. Yet, with its thatched roof and slatted wooden belfry, it has a curious charm that is all its own.

The original chapel, built of corrugated iron, was erected in 1894, by Lord North's daughter, the Hon. Mrs. Benyon. Before then, local catholics said Mass at Lord North's Wroxton Abbey, which had its own chapel and chaplain. By 1948, the old corrugated iron chapel had fallen into such a sad state of disrepair, that it had become an eyesore. It was Canon Wall who organised a group of laity to set about restoring it. Glass taken from churches bombed in the war was used to provide new windows, and the roof was completely re-thatched with Norfolk reed. A new statue of St. Thomas of Canterbury was commissioned for the front porch, and as a tribute to the chapel's restorer, its features were modelled on Canon Wall.

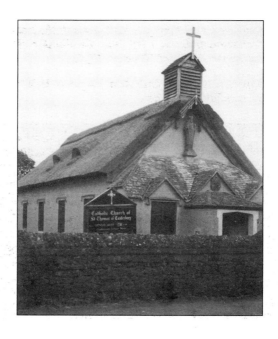

WROXTON

WROXTON ABBEY – HOME OF A RELUCTANT PRIME MINISTER

Location:	Wroxton Village – On A422, 2 miles north west of Banbury.
Access:	Though not open to the public, the house can be admired from the grounds to which the public is freely admitted.

Following the dissolution of the monasteries by Henry VIII, Wroxton Priory was bought by Sir Thomas Pope, who gave it to Trinity College, Oxford. He did, however, retain a lifetime tenancy for his brother John, and his heirs. About 1618, John's son, Sir William Pope, built the first part of the grand Jacobean mansion that stands on the site today. It is perhaps interesting to reflect that Wroxton Abbey, destroyed by Henry VIII, was rebuilt by – a Pope!

Through the marriage of Lady Frances Pope to Francis, 1st Earl of Guilford, the house passed to the North family. Their son was Lord Frederick North, the reluctant Prime Minister to George III at the time of American Independence. Despite losing the American Colonies, North's white marble monument in the village church reflects the glorious age when Britannia ruled the waves and the British Lion ruled much of the world. Wroxton remained the home of the North family until 1932. In 1963, Trinity College sold the house to Farleigh Dickinson University of America, who now call it Wroxton College.

If you have the energy, you might enjoy a walk through the park to see the dovecote built by Sanderson Miller in 1745, and the obelisk erected to commemorate a visit by the Prince of Wales in 1739.

Opposite the Abbey gates is the 'The North Arms'; a pretty little inn with a thatched roof and a sundial over its door.

WROXTON

A MOST UNUSUAL SIGNPOST

> *Location:*   On A422 Banbury – Stratford Road at the North Newington turn.

About a half mile from the village of Wroxton is a most unusual and interesting signpost. Made of Hornton stone, each of its four sides bears two sculptured hands pointing the traveller in the direction indicated. The hands are those of a man and a woman, each identifiable by a ring on a finger. There has been a guide post on this site since 1686, when the first one was placed there by Mr. Fran White. Time and the weather took their toll, and it was the public-spirited Wroxton, Balscote and Drayton Preservation Society that raised the money to pay for its renovation in 1974. The work was skilfully executed by Mr. George Carter, a local stonemason. Using the original stone, he chipped three quarters of an inch off the face to make it clean for recarving. In addition to the sculptured hands, he embellished the corners with acorns, oak leaves, and old English roses.

As well as being a signpost, it also serves as a sundial; but this is no ordinary sundial. When it was dismantled for renovation, Mr. Mark Taylor, an authority on sundials, noticed it had been deliberately set off-square to the plinth so that the east face was at 187 degrees, allowing 7 degrees for magnetic and true variations to give the correct 180 degree reading.

STEEPLE ASTON

HOPCROFT'S HOLT – THE GHOSTLY HAUNT OF HIGHWAYMEN

Location:	On A4260 (formerly A423), 10 miles north of Oxford.
Access:	Open to the public.

The inn sign at Hopcroft's Holt is of a highwayman on a horse, brandishing a loaded pistol. Behind him, a noose hangs from a gallows, warning of the fate that awaited him. This is no ordinary highwayman, but the infamous Claude Duval, who lay in wait for victims at these lonely crossroads. Travellers were terrorised by the black-masked bandit peering in at the window of their coach, brandishing a loaded pistol and demanding – 'Your money or your life!' He was finally caught and hanged at Tyburn.

You might think that was the end of Duval; but no. Hopcroft's Holt is reputedly Oxfordshire's most haunted inn. Though his mortal remains lie safely buried in the churchyard at Covent Garden, it is said that Duval's evil ghost still roams the inn. Towards the end of the 18th century, some years after the highwayman was hanged, the landlord, Spurrier and his wife were brutally murdered. His body was found on the site of the staircase; she was found slumped in a chair by the inglenook fireplace. They never did find out who did it; whoever it was didn't leave any clues. But everyone suspects it was the ghost of Claude Duval.

Ghostly happenings have often been reported over the centuries. In the 1950s, a lady told of the ghost of a Cavalier she had seen near the Inn. More recently, there was the strange experience of the landlord Alan Sandell and his wife, Pam. On an August night in 1976, both were asleep in bed when she was awakened by an eerie presence in the room. She opened her eyes, and although it was totally dark, she could see the outline of things in the room. Petrified, her heart stopped beating as she saw the shadowy figure of a man bending over the bed. At first she thought it might be her husband, and called out his name. There was no response, so she switched on the bedside light. Her husband was lying beside her in bed, still sleeping. The mysterious figure disappeared without trace. They were not unused to the ghostly presence; both they and the staff had heard mysterious voices and footsteps. One night, Mr.Sandell decided to investigate for himself, and with his dog, climbed the winding staircase. On reaching the unused attic at the top of the inn, he heared footsteps crossing the attic floor. The dog growled and his hackles rose as he stood rooted to the floor.

Hopcroft's Holt dates from the late 17th century, when a house, which later became a coaching inn stood on the site. It is still a popular place for travellers, and though now modernised, it still retains its mysterious character and haunting charm.

WOODSTOCK

BLENHEIM PALACE – A RICH REWARD FOR A CONQUERING HERO

Location: Woodstock.

Access: The Palace is open daily 10.30am-5.30pm, mid-March to the end of October. The Park is open 9am-5pm throughout the year.

'The finest view in England' was how Lady Randolph Churchill described her first sight of Blenheim. It is the view of palace and parkland, with the Grand Bridge spanning the lake, that visitors get as they enter the park through the Triumphal Arch. The scene, painted by Turner, caused George III to exclaim 'We have nothing to equal this.'

As a reward for his illustrious service to the nation, Queen Anne gave John Churchill, 1st Duke of Marlborough, the Royal Manor of Woodstock, in 1704, and signified that she would build him a house at her own expense. The house was to be called Blenheim, after the Danube village where Marlborough achieved his greatest victory over the forces of Louis XIV.

After some disagreement with his Duchess about the choice of architect, the Duke commissioned John Vanburgh, who was then an assistant to Sir Christopher Wren. The country's finest craftsmen were employed to build the Palace, among them Grinling Gibbons and Edward Strongs, who had worked on St. Paul's Cathedral. Building started in 1705, and the house was completed by 1722.

One hundred and fifty-two years later, Blenheim Palace was to be associated with another famous Churchill, when on the 30th November 1874, Winston Leonard Spencer Churchill was born there.

Monument to John Vanburgh, Blenheim Palace.

Triumphal Gate, Blenheim Palace.

WOODSTOCK

WHERE WINSTON PROPOSED TO CLEMMIE

> *Location:*   Temple of Diana, Blenheim Palace Arboretum.

The stone-built Temple of Diana, is built on classical Greek lines, supported by Doric columns. It commands a superb view of the lake and is a perfectly romantic setting. In the summer of 1908, the Temple was the scene of a special romance, when young Winston Churchill and Miss Clementine Hozier were weekend house guests of the Duke of Marborough. They were walking together in the garden when a sudden shower of rain drove them to shelter in the Temple. It was while they were waiting for the rain to pass that Winston proposed to Clementine.

To mark European Architectural Heritage Year in 1975, the Temple was restored by the present Duke, who invited Lady Churchill to unveil a commemorative plaque. She recalled 'There was a bench there then, and as I sat there with Winston, I watched a beetle slowly moving across the floor. 'If that beetle reaches that crack,' I said to myself, 'and Winston hasn't proposed, then he isn't going to.' But he did propose!' He later wrote: 'At Blenheim, I took two very important decisions – to be born and to marry. I am happily content with the decisions I took on both those occasions'.

64

WOODSTOCK

VANBRUGH'S GRAND EXTRAVAGANZA

> *Location:* Blenheim Palace.

The Grand Bridge spanning the lake at Blenheim is a remarkable architectural extravaganza. It was originally designed to cross a marshy vale through which the River Glyme flows. The Duke of Marlborough's architect, Vanbrugh, saw it as an opportunity to build the finest bridge in Europe, but he was opposed from the outset by the Duchess. 'I made Mr. Vanbrugh my enemy by the constant disputes I had with him to prevent his extravagance.' She complained to her friends that it contained no less than thirty-three rooms, and had a house in each corner. But she did concede that it was much prettier than London Bridge. According to the Palace Guide Book, 'Some of the rooms have fireplaces and chimneys, and one large windowless chamber has been plastered and fitted with an elliptical arch as though for a theatre.'

The river flowed in three canals beneath the bridge, cascading through the central arch into a pool on the western side. It was after the death of the Duchess in 1744, that Lancelot 'Capability' Brown was brought in to landscape the park and build the magnificent lake we see today.

WOODSTOCK

MARLBOROUGH'S TRIUMPHAL COLUMN OF VICTORY

Location:	Blenheim Park.

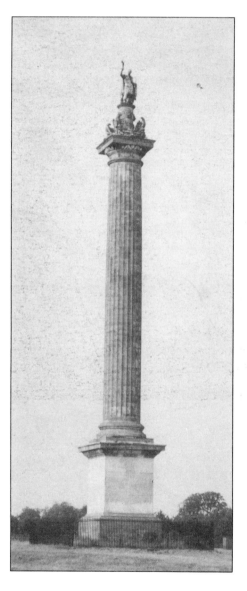

From the top of the Column of Victory high above Blenheim, John Churchill, 1st Duke of Marborough, surveys his earthly estate 134 feet below. This magnificent Doric column depicting him as a Roman General surrounded by eagles, was erected in 1730, eight years after his death. The site was chosen by his Duchess, who also chose Henry St. John, 1st Viscount Bolingbroke, to write a lengthy tribute to the Duke, inscribed on the side of the plinth facing the Palace. In his Life Of Marlborough, Sir Winston Churchill described the incription as a masterpiece which '. . . would serve as a history in itself, were all other records lost.' The other three sides of the plinth are filled with an inscription of the Act Of Parliament 'For the better Enabling of Her Majesty to grant the Honour and Manor of Woodstock with the Hundred of Wootton to the Duke of Marlborough and his Heirs in Consideration of the Eminent Services by him Performed to Her Majesty and the Publick.'

'And everybody praised the Duke,
Who this great fight did win.
'But what good came of it at last?'
Quoth little Peterkin.
'Why that I cannot tell' said he,
'But 'twas a famous victory.'

(The Battle of Blenheim by Robert Southey.)

BLADON

THE GRAVES OF WINSTON CHURCHILL AND HIS FAMILY

Location: St. Martin's Churchyard, Bladon.

A large slice of Britain's history lies buried at Bladon. St.Martin's was a little-known country church until the 30th January 1964. On that day, the body of Sir Winston Churchill was brought from the pomp and ceremony of a state funeral in St. Pauls Cathedral, to rest in this humble village churchyard. His father Randolph and Jennie, his mother, were already buried here, as were his daughters Marigold and Diana, and his brother Jack. His son Randolph, who died in 1968, and his talented actress daughter Sarah, who died in 1982 are also buried here. Lady Churchill survived Sir Winston until her death in 1977, She now rests with him in the grave at Bladon, that has become a place of pilgrimage for people from all over the world.

ISLIP

PORTRAIT OF EDWARD THE CONFESSOR

Location:	St. Nicholas Church.

I have given to Christ and to S. Peter in Westminster ye little town of Islippe coberein I was born with all the things which belong thereunto

'I have given to Christ and St. Peter in Westminster ye little town of Islippe wherein I was born.' Thus reads an extract from the Will of Edward the Confessor, beneath a full-length portrait in the north aisle of Islip Church. Builder of Westminster Abbey, Edward endowed it with buildings and land in Islip where he was born in 1004. The Abbot of Westminster was granted the privilege of nominating the rectors of Islip. This passed to the Dean of Westminster after the dissolution.

Above Saint Edward's portrait, is what looks like a death mask. It was placed there by a former rector and generous village benefactor, Dr. Robert South, and is thought to be of Dr. Richard Busby, his former headmaster at Westminster School.

Though there is evidence of a church in Islip in Saxon times, the present one dates from the 12th and 14th centuries, with the tower being added in the 15th century. On the 28th February, 1645, Oliver Cromwell watched the battle of Islip Bridge from the tower, when his troops defeated the Royalists.

BECKLEY

ST. MARY'S CHURCH – 14TH CENTURY WALL PAINTINGS

Location: Off B4027, south east of Islip.

Access: Open during normal church hours.

Beckley is one of the villages around Otmoor that comprise the Seven Towns. Set on rising ground, it enjoys lovely views of the marshland below. The summer air is heavy with the fragrance of old-fashioned roses that grow in the gardens of quaint thatched cottages.

The present church dates mainly from the 14th century, though there is evidence of an earlier church. Of particular interest are the wall paintings, dating from the 14th century, revealed in the restoration of 1845. The 15th century painting above the tower, is of the Last Judgement, depicting Christ In Majesty. St. Mary, to whom the church is dedicated is seen with John the Baptist, interceding for departed souls. Tiny naked figures rise from their tombs as the devil dances with his catch net at the ready. The Arms of George III have been superimposed on a blocked-up opening in the tower. Below, St. Peter holds the Papal Staff opposite St. Paul who carries a sword. There are older paintings on other walls of the church, and a good description of them is to be found in the Church Guide. This charming church is steeped in history and over countless generations has been adapted to the needs of the day. The wooden Jacobean pulpit, now stripped of its paint, is worthy of notice, as is the font, the parish chest, and the iron work on the south door, all early 13th century.

CHARLTON ON OTMOOR

MAIDENS GARLAND

Location: Two miles north east of Islip.

There is a beautifully-preserved early sixteenth century rood-screen in the church of St. Mary the Virgin at Charlton on Otmoor. It was originally adorned on either side by statues of St.John and The Virgin Mary, but following the Reformation, these were replaced by less controversial garlands. Dunkin's History of 1823 illustrates these garlands, and records that 'The rood-loft shows two large hooped garlands of flowers, appropriately surmounted with crosses.' In 1854, the Rev.George Riggs had the garlands removed from the screen during alterations. This was clearly against most people's wishes for as soon as he left the village, the congregation replaced them. Today there is just one large garland cross made from box clippings. It is placed on the rood-screen on May Day each year, when in accordance with custom, the village children make tiny wooden crosses which they cover with flowers and take to the church. The children also make garlands of flowers to put on the screen.

STANTON ST. JOHN

BIRTHPLACE OF JOHN WHITE, FOUNDER OF MASSACHUSETTS U.S.A.

Location: Opposite St. John's Church.
No Access – privately owned.

An inscription above the door of a grey stone cottage opposite the church at Stanton St. John records the birthplace of John White (1575-1648), Fellow of New College Oxford and Chief Founder of the Colony of Massachusetts, New England.

John White was baptised at Stanton St. John on 6th January 1575. Educated at Winchester, he was elected a Fellow of New College, Oxford in 1595. In 1606, he went to Dorchester in Dorset to become Rector of Holy Trinity. A moderate puritan, he worked hard to improve the lives of the people by finding work for the able poor. He used the local brewhouse profits to maintain those unable to work due to sickness and infirmity. Known as the Patriarch of Dorchester, he was instrumental in sending men from Dorset to Massachusetts to establish the Dorset Colony '. . . where such as were nonconformist might enjoy liberty of conscience.' He was instrumental in getting the New England Council to sign the Massachusetts Patent, confirmed by Royal Charter on 4th March 1629. He died on 21st July 1648, and is buried in St. Peter's Chapel, Dorchester.

THAME

THE BIRDCAGE INN

Location:	Upper High Street.
Access:	Normal licensing hours.

With records of its existence dating from 1430, the black and white half-timbered Birdcage Inn is perhaps best known as Thame's oldest pub. It has in its time been variously used as a prison, and a place for lepers, who were kept isolated in an upper room and fed through a trapdoor by nuns. A notorious thief known as 'Magpie' was once held here. When word of his incarceration got about, the locals said 'the bird is in his cage' – henceforth it was known as the Birdcage Inn. During the Napoleonic hostilities, 120 French prisoners of war were held in Thame; 16 in the cellar of the Birdcage Inn. Whilst in captivity, the prisoners were allowed their freedom in town during the day; and even formed their own masonic lodge. Though a few absconded, several took a liking to Thame and decided to stay; some even married local girls. In more recent years, the inn has gained a reputation for being haunted by the ghost of a leper who was imprisoned at the Inn before being stoned to death.

THAME

A MOTHER'S SAD MEMORIAL TO HER CHILDREN

Location:	Parish churchyard. Situated immediately to the right as you go through the gate.

There are many graves in Thame churchyard. Some are quite recent, but others have stood there for so many years, that any trace of who lies beneath has long since been erased from the stones by the weather. In the shade of a tree, one sad little stone stands apart from the rest. Surprisingly, its simple inscription, embellished by leaves and a gruesome skull, has survived the ravages of more than three centuries' weather.

> *'Heare Lies Neare Two of my children Deare*
> *Robert aged 2 years 10 mon Mary 2 days 1668.'*

Its sheer simplicity prompts one to wonder why they died so young, and who the broken hearted parent might have been.

73

THAME

RYCOTE – A CHAPEL ROYAL

Location:	3 miles south west of Thame, off A329.
Access:	Open to visitors: occasional Mondays from April to September inclusive.
Enquiries to:	English Heritage. Tel: 01305-860853 & 01272-750700.

The setting of Rycote Chapel is of tranquil beauty. Built in 1449 by Richard Quartermaine, it is all that remains of a large medieval estate. The manor of Rycote was bought by Sir John Williams, a guardian of the young Princess who, as Queen Elizabeth I, was a frequent visitor to Rycote. Later, both James I and Charles I came here. The manor was destroyed by fire in 1745, and only the stable block, now a private residence, survived.

A fine yew tree stands on the lawn in front of the chapel, said to have been planted in 1135 to commemorate the coronation of King Stephen. According to legend, it was brought from the Holy Land, and used as a pilgrim marker on the nearby Oxfordshire Way. The plain architecture of the chapel's exterior belies the simple beauty of what you will find within. Beneath the original waggon-vaulted roof are square wooden pews put there when the chapel was built. A curious feature is a fireplace against the north wall, with a flue built into the buttress outside. It is thought to have been used for baking wafers used for mass. The two-tier family pew is remarkable for its painted panels and exquisitely carved screen. Opposite is the Royal Pew, built for Charles I in 1625, when Court and Parliament moved from London to Oxford to escape the plague.

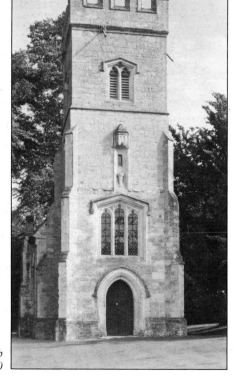

Rycote Chapel. (Courtesy of English Heritage Photographic Library)

Rycote Chapel interior. (Courtesy of English Heritage Photographic Library)

WHEATLEY

THE VILLAGE LOCK-UP

Location: Off A40, 3 miles east of Oxford.

Set at a junction on the High Street at Wheatley is a curious pyramid-shaped stone edifice topped by a stone ball. Devoid of windows, the only access is by a wooden door, and the casual visitor might wonder why so strange a building should occupy such a prominent position at the centre of the village. Dating back to the early 1800s, this was the village lock-up, long since redundant. It was a secure repository and a sobering place in which offenders could spend the night and reflect on their misdemeanours.

Reminding us of the far-off days – and chilling nights of the body snatchers, an interesting tombstone in Wheatley's churchyard carries a grim warning.

Stay, reader stay, remove me not from this tomb
Before thou hast considered well thy doome
My Bowe stands Ready Bent & couldst thou but see
My Arrows drawn to the head and Arms of Thee
Stay wandring guest, Take home with thee this Line,
The Grave that next is opened may be Thine.

GREAT HASELEY

AN OLD WINDMILL IN NEED OF A FRIEND!

Location: Off A329, eight miles east of Oxford.

On the way from Rycote to Great Milton you will pass through Great Haseley where, standing forlorn in a field not far from the road, is a derelict windmill. A date mark on the side suggests it was built in 1807, though it is thought it dates back to 1760. The mill was still working at the time of the First World War, but later it fell into disuse. Some renovation was carried out in the 1970s, but now, after years of neglect, only the rooks fly in and out of its open windows. The basic fabric is good, and all it seems to need is a generous friend to restore it. Perhaps the National Lottery or Millennium Fund could come to the rescue!

GREAT MILTON

1939 – DAD'S ARMY PIKES

Location: Village Church.

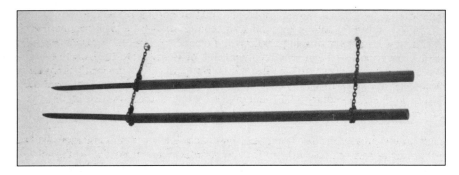

It is said that we British are blessed with a capacity to laugh at ourselves; never more apparent than in the old favourite television comedy, 'Dad's Army'. The younger generation might well ask – 'did they really get up to all those funny antics during the war?' For those of us who remember the far off days of the 1940's, the answer is a resounding 'Yes!' In the early days of the war, 'Dad's Army' was known as the Local Defence Volunteers. They didn't have uniforms at first; just a khaki coloured arm band bearing the black letters L.D.V. Neither did

they have guns, and history portrays them as elderly men armed with a motley collection of weapons ranging from hay forks, to pick-axe handles. They clearly had a sense of history at Great Milton, where in St. Peter's Church, two long handled pikes have been preserved for posterity. These were officially issued to the local Home Guard, as 'Dad's Army' was later called, to repel the expected German invasion. Fortunately, they were never put to the test, and they now hang high on a wall above the 17th century tomb of Sir Michael Dormer. One wonders whether 'Dad's Army might not have been better armed with Sir Michael's helmet and sword that hang on the opposite wall!

Locked in a glass case on the west wall of the church are two historic instruments; a serpent shaped ophicleide key bugle, and a clarinet. They were played by members of the church band that provided the music for services in the 1800s – strains of Thomas Hardy!! The players sat in a gallery at the west end of the church, now long since demolished.

GREAT MILTON

LE MANOIR – MAINTAINING THE ENTENTE CORDIALE

> *Location:*   Le Manoir aux Quat' Saisons.

Adjacent to the church is an elegant stone built manor house, with a distinguished history dating from the 13th century. In 1416, it was occupied by Sir Thomas Camoys, a dashing soldier and favourite of Richard II. Some years earlier, Sir Thomas brought the intended bride of Henry IV to England from Brittany, and was given £100 for his efforts. But perhaps his greatest achievement was to be at Agincourt with Henry V. William Radwyld rebuilt and enlarged the Manor in the 15th century, and a hundred years later, it was bought by Sir Reginald Dormer, a wealthy wool merchant.

Early in the present century, the house was again improved and enlarged. Its last private owner was the Hon.David Bewicke-Copley, who succeeded to the title Lord Cromwell in 1966. After his death in 1982, Lady Cromwell sold the house, and in March 1984, the celebrated French Restaurateur Monsieur Raymond Blanc opened the doors of Le Manoir aux Quat' Saisons. Acknowleged as one of Britain's finest restaurants, it has an international reputation for elegance, comfort and exceptional cuisine. In magnificent grounds, with 17th century water gardens, the medieval dovecote of Cotswold stone, is now the honeymoon suite; perhaps maintaining a long tradition of billing and cooing!

Like many historic houses Le Manoir had a ghost. Lady Cromwell had a premonition that her husband might not have wished her to sell the house after his death, and strange things started to happen. Bedding was mysteriously turned down and curtains pulled back in the master bedroom. Mysterious marks were found in the bath and shower. Thinking perhaps that the late Lord Cromwell was expressing his displeasure, his widow brought in a priest to exorcise the unhappy presence, and thereafter all was well.

GARSINGTON

GLORIOUS GARSINGTON – AN OPERATIC JACOBEAN MANOR

> *Location:*   Off the B480, two miles east of the Oxford ring road.
>
> No regular public access to the house or grounds.

Garsington Manor is a small Jacobean mansion, circa 1630, built of grey stone, and set in a gravelled court yard between high yew hedges. Lady Ottoline and Phillp Morrell went to live there during the first World War, and it soon became a favourite haunt of the Bloomsbury set. Bertrand Russell, Virginia Woolf, T. S. Eliot, Lawrence, Sassoon and Huxley, and a host of other literary and intellectual luminaries came to stay and indulge in lively conversation. In recent years, Garsington has earned an enviable reputation for its annual Opera Festival which lasts three weeks from mid-June. Staged on the terrace, the audience is seated in a heated auditorium. Performances start in the evening at 6.15 and end just after 10pm, with a civilised interval for dinner. Time for concert guests to wander in the exquisite flower gardens, dine in the Barn Restaurant or, if the weather is propitious, to take a hamper and enjoy a romantic picnic. Recent productions have included Mozart's 'Don Giovanni', Haydn's 'Il Mondo della Luna' and Rossini's 'Il Barbiere di Siviglia', all acclaimed enthusiastically in the national press. No wonder there is a waiting list to become a 'Friend'. (Details of the Festival can be obtained by telephoning the Box Office on 01865-361545.)

GARSINGTON

A CHURCH CLOCK WITH ONLY ONE HAND

Just along the road from Garsington Manor, is the village church of St. Mary which is well worth a visit. Its most interesting feature is the clock, installed in 1796 at a cost of £172.4s. The clock has two faces on the north and south walls of the tower, with a single minute hand on each face. The time is marked in quarter hours, and a tenor bell chimes every hour. Above the vestry in the bell tower, a very large pendulum with a soothing tick swings slowly to and fro.

CHALGROVE FIELD

WHERE PARLIAMENT'S PATRIOT JOHN HAMPDEN FELL

Location: Off A470 Watlington (4 miles) to Oxford road.

'Chalgrove Field? The battle was afoor my day zur.' The old man didn't know much about the war. But he could remember John Hampden's monument being put up in 1843. Over the years, the plough has turned up human bones in the fields,and they even found a cannon ball stuck in a tree at Chiselhampton.

But who was this John Hampden whose monument stands on Chalgrove Field? For the answer, we must return to the 18th June 1643, when England was at war with itself. It was a bright and sunny Sunday morning, as church bells rang to summon the faithful to prayer. In a field of corn nearby, Prince Rupert's Royalist troops faced Cromwell's men, with pikes and swords at the ready. Though Royalists outnumbered the Roundheads, Colonel Hampden rode into the fray ahead of his Greencoats. Hardly had pikes and swords locked in battle when Hampden fell, mortally wounded, shot from behind by a Royalist trooper. Two shots had penetrated deep into his shoulder, and he was seen to ride from the field of battle. He rode five miles to Thame, where surgeons took two balls of shot from his shoulder. They dressed his wound, but to no avail, for he died on 24th June. A locket he was wearing at the time of his death contained a cryptic note: 'Against my King I do not fight, but for my King and kingdom's right.'

To the solemn sound of muffled drums, bareheaded troops carrying furled flags draped with black ribbon, followed Hampden's coffin to its burial in Great Hampden Church. But doubts persisted as to whether Hampden's mortal wound was inflicted by the enemy, or whether, as had been asserted, his own pistol had accidentally burst and shattered his hand. In 1828 the lead coffin containing his remains was disinterred, and placed in the centre of the church. There, in the presence of the rector and a silent assemblage, it was opened by the village plumber. The right hand was missing from the arm, and the bones indicated that it had been sawn off. On searching beneath the shroud a number of bones from a hand were found wrapped in a cloth. Thereafter it was concluded that his death had been accidental. He was reinterred next to his wife in a grave near the west window.

CHALGROVE AIRFIELD – STATION 465

UNITED STATES ARMY AIR FORCE MEMORIAL

Location: Off A470 Watlington (4 miles) to Oxford road.

Like Hampden's Civil War battlefield, Chalgrove Airfield is quiet now. Not so very long ago, its rural peace was shattered by the noise of aircraft taking off and landing; or sometimes simply taking off, never to return. From here in the second World War, men of American Photographic Reconnaissance, known as the 'Eyes of the 8th' United States Army Air Force, flew to occupied Europe. With the Pathfinder Paratroops stationed here, they were part of the spearhead to liberate Europe. Now, by the quiet cross-roads near Hampden's monument, a smaller modest memorial plaque commemorates the brave young men of Chalgrove Airfield. 'May They Never Be Forgotten'.

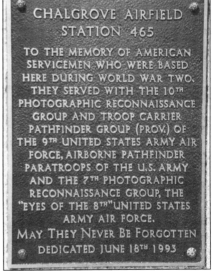

EWELME

EWELME CHURCH – THE MEDIEVAL WORLD OF THE CHAUCERS

Access: Open during normal church hours.

Ewelme is magnificently medieval. To pass through the quadrangle of its ancient almshouses and enter the church of St. Mary the Virgin, is to step back centuries into the world of the Chaucers. Thomas, son of Geoffrey, author of the Canterbury Tales, lies with his wife Matilda in an altar tomb, richly embellished with colourful medieval shields of arms, said to be the finest on any tomb in England.

Close by, is the sublimely beautiful alabaster tomb of the poet's grand-daughter Alice. A lady of rank and influence, she was twice widowed, first by the death in 1428 of Thomas Montacute, Earl of Salisbury, who was killed at Orleans by a well-aimed cannon ball that struck him full in the face. Her second widowhood was caused by the death of William de la Pole, Duke of Suffolk, whose head was hacked off with a rusty sword in 1450.

Beneath a canopy, elaborately carved from a single piece of alabaster, her effigy, dressed in the austere habit of a nun, lies in an attitude of prayer. Wearing a ducal coronet, her head rests on a cushion supported by angels, and on her left forearm she wears the Order of the Garter. It is said that before her coronation, Queen Victoria sent to Ewelme to determine how the ribbon should be worn by a woman. Queen Mary also took this as evidence of how Ladies of the Order should wear the Garter. Under the tomb, a 'memento mori' is a grim reminder of what lies inside, and a testimony to the leveller that is the grave.

In the churchyard is the grave of the celebrated author Jerome K. Jerome, whose simple tombstone is in sharp contrast to the grandeur of the tombs inside the church.

Thomas Chaucer's Tomb, Ewelme Church.

Tomb of Alice, Duchess of Suffolk, Ewelme Church.

85

EWELME

THE MEDIEVAL ALMSHOUSES

Leaving the church by the west door you descend a few steps to the almshouses. Built of red brick and set in a quadrangle, they were, it is said, originally inhabited by thirteen survivors of Agincourt, and this might well be true for it is known for certain that fifteen local men fought in the battle.

EWELME

THE OLDEST CHURCH PRIMARY SCHOOL IN BRITAIN

The children of Ewelme can proudly boast that theirs is the oldest Church School in the State system. It was founded in 1437, when a Grammar Master was appointed to educate the village children '. . . freely without exaccion of any School hire.' The school was built about 1450, and like many village schools, consisted of a simple hall. Its doors were originally the west doors of the church, and are an impressive example of medieval craftsmanship. So too is the original timber roof, still in an excellent state of preservation. Although the interior has been updated over the centuries, its original red brick external appearance has, like the almshouses, remained unaltered. A small room over the porch, used by generations of Grammar Masters is still used by the school's Headmaster.

The Primary School, Ewelme.

NETTLEBED

AMERICAN ARMY'S MINIATURE CASTLE

> *Location:* B481 Stoke Row to Nettlebed Road, opposite Merrimoles Farm, half a mile from Nettlebed.

You could easily miss the miniature castle if you didn't know it was there. Standing incongruously and almost hidden in the trees by the side of the road, nobody seems to know why it was put there. The only clue is in the inscription over its gate: '1942 343 Engineers U.S. Army'. It remains one of the unsolved mysteries of the Second World War. Apart from many passers-by who find it a curious object of interest, it is still a place of pilgrimage for returning American servicemen who were stationed in the area during the Second World War.

NETTLEBED
THE LAST BRICK KILN

> *Location:*   Kiln Close, just past the Watlington road.

Bricks and tiles have been made at Nettlebed since the Middle Ages. The earliest records date from 1365 when 35,000 tiles were made for Wallingford Castle. In 1416 Michael Warwick was paid £40 for 200,000 'brykes', and £15 for delivering them three miles from the kiln at Crocker End to Stonor House. The accounts at

Stonor House refer to 'lez Flemyngges' who came with their skills from the Low Countries. The Flemish style is particularly noticeable in Ewelme's almshouses and primary school. The names of tilemakers, potters and brickmakers, as well as kilnsmen and women are recorded in the parish registers and census returns of Nettlebed, Crocker End and Rotherfield Greys.

Of the five known kiln sites in the county, there remain few traces of the brickyards, drying sheds and tramways or even the clay pits that supplied them. Nettlebed is perhaps unique in preserving some traces of its industry. Its interesting bottle-shaped kiln, stands incongruously next to an unsightly lamp post, surrounded by modern houses. But it is worth going to see! So too is John Piper's window in St. Bartholomew's Church; placed there in 1970.

HENLEY ON THAMES

THE FACES ON HENLEY BRIDGE

There has been a bridge over the Thames at Henley since time immemorial, and from all accounts it has had a chequered and sometimes turbulent history. Mention was made of it in 1230 when eight bishops granted indulgences to its benefactors. In 1501 two arches were added, and in 1514, mention is made of a chapel on the bridge dedicated to St. Anne, together with a granary and dwelling-houses and an inn. During the Civil War the bridge suffered at the hands of both Royalist and Roundheads. By 1754, it had become dangerous, and on 12th March of that year, was swept away in the floods. A flood-mark on the Red Lion Hotel recorded 'In the flood in 1774 on March ye 11 the Thames rose to this stone.'

In 1786, a new bridge of Headington stone was built costing £10,000. It was much admired by Horace Walpole who wrote '. . . for grace it does not vail the bonnet to the Ponte de Trinita in Florence.' It is the elegant bridge we see today, and of particular interest are the sculptured heads on the keystones on either side. The bearded countenance of Thamesis stares downstream, while the classical features of Isis gaze upstream where according to legend, both rivers were united in marriage. The sculpture is the work of General Seymour Conway's talented daughter the Hon Mrs. Anne Damer. Surprisingly, she was friendly with Nelson and Napoleon, both of whom she sculptured. She was also friendly with the Freemans of Fawley Court, whose daughter was her model for the face of Isis.

The Face of Isis, Henley Bridge.

HENLEY ON THAMES

TEMPLE ISLAND

Location:	Cross Henley Bridge on the A423 and take the first left for Remenham. At Remenham follow the river footpath downstream.
Access:	No public access.

Temple Island, also known as Fawley Island on the River Thames at Henley, is familiar to rowing enthusiasts as the starting point for the Royal Regatta. Visitors during the rest of the year will see it as a pretty little island in the middle of the Thames, and wonder what its history might be. Built in 1771, the neo-Classical Island Temple was designed by James Wyatt, as a summer house for Sambrooke Freeman of Fawley Court. Surmounted by an elegant cupola with a marble statue of a lady inside, it had one room, beautifully decorated with frescoes in the Etruscan style; the earliest example in England. The statue was replaced in recent years after the original had been taken by pranksters during the 1954 regatta. It seems that a rowing crew, knocked out of the regatta, removed the statue during the night to take it by punt to the judge's box at the end of the course. Not surprisingly, it proved too heavy, and was dropped in the water where it stayed for several years until found by workmen dredging the river bed. By now, its place in the cupola had been taken by a marble figure of Bacchante, of exactly the same size and date as the original. In 1853, a four-bedroomed cottage was added to the temple to accomodate overnight visitors, but in recent years it has been used by the resident caretaker.

By the early 1950s, the temple was in a sad state of dilapidation. Much concern was voiced in the press, and appeals were made to the County Council to save it. Designated a building of historic and architectural interest, the future of the island and its temple was secured in 1987. by Mr. & Mrs. Alan Burrough, who in an act of public spirited generosity, enabled Henley Royal Regatta to acquire a 999 year lease. During the following three years the temple was carefully restored, and is now available for hire as the perfect setting for corporate hospitality, business meetings and private parties. Details are available from: Henley Royal Regatta – Tel: 01491-572153 or Fax 01491-575509.

HENLEY ON THAMES

THE WANDERING OBELISK

Location: Mill Meadow.

To look at the grey stone obelisk by the river in Mill Meadow, you might think it had always been there; but not so. Earliest records tell of its standing near Middle Row in Hart Street. In those early days it was known as 'the pump', because a pump used for washing the streets was attached to it. Following the demolition of Middle Row in the 1790s, it was moved to the town centre cross-roads, where it was erected, minus the pump. Here, it was used as a milestone until 1885, when it was moved to make room for the Phillimore Fountain. Its new site was at the junction of Marlow Road and Northfield End, where this time it served as a lamp post. By the early 1970s, the time had come for the obelisk to move yet again. The problem was, where to put it? In an imaginative attempt to solve the problem, a model was made and tried out in various parts of the town. To the amusement of some and irritation of others, Mr. David Crossman, a member of the Town Council, composed a light-hearted biographical poem which, it was suggested, should be engraved on a plaque and attached to the obelisk. This generated a heated debate in Council, with one member suggesting the obelisk be sold to the Americans. Happily, that suggestion was not pursued, and the obelisk finally found a permanent (?) riverside home in Mill Meadow. And what of the poem? Well it might be worth repeating here just for posterity.

ODE TO AN OBELISK

'Upon here placed, at much risk
The history of this obelisk.
Once it stood in Middle Row,
In front of the Catherine Wheel, you know;
Out of it did water gush,
The dirty streets it used to flush.
At this time this granite lump,
Was known to all just as 'the pump'.
When Middle Row was taken down,
It went to the centre of the town.
On it hung two lamps of lead,
And from it distances were read.
Its third move was to Northfield End,
Near Rupert's Elm on the bend.
But when they built a roundabout,
The obelisk again moved out.
And now it stands upon this spot,
But for such purpose as we know not what.'

STOKE ROW

THE MAHARAJAH'S WELL

Location:	Stoke Row, Henley on Thames.
Access:	Open daily throughout the year.

The Maharajah's Well must surely be one of the most intriguing curiosities in the County of Oxfordshire. Exotic and oriental in appearance, it stands splendid and incongruous amid trimmed lawns and well-kept gardens in the Chiltern village of Stoke Row. Its origin can be traced to a land dispute between two brothers in the Indian village of Azimgurgh in 1831. The dispute was settled by Edward Anderdon Read, the son of a Chiltern squire who was serving with the East India Company. He assumed ownership of the disputed land on which he sunk a much-needed well for the village.

Some years later he related the story of the well to the Maharajah of Benares, adding that the people of his own community in the Chilterns suffered from the same kind of water deprivation. The Maharajah remembered this when in 1862, he wanted to make an endowment in England. He wrote to Mr. Reade who gladly accepted the generous gift, which was used to provide a well for the village.

The well itself is no less impressive than the ornate edifice that stands above it. Four feet wide, it was sunk to a depth of 368 feet; more than twice the height of Nelson's Column, and greater than the height of St. Paul's Cathedral. Every bit was hand excavated by men who dug down until they could dig no further. It was dirty, damp and dangerous work in rancid air, with the opening above becoming little more than a pin prick of light. The well was opened to celebrate Queen Victoria's birthday, on the 24th May 1864, just a year after work had begun.

An excellent illustrated history of the Maharajah's Well can be purchased at Well Cottage.

The Maharajah's Well.

WELL COTTAGE

| *Location:* | Stoke Row, Henley on Thames. |

Visitors to the Maharajah's Well will be no less intrigued and charmed by the tiny red brick octagonal-shaped cottage that stands close by. More like a summer house than a cottage, it was built at a cost of £74.14.6, to house the Well Warden. It consists of a single storey with a lovely little chimney in the centre of the roof. Inside, are three tiny rooms, a living room, bedroom and kitchen.

DIDCOT

DIDCOT RAILWAY CENTRE – RE-CREATING THE GOLDEN AGE OF STEAM

Location:	Adjacent to Didcot Parkway Station.
Access:	Open weekends all year and daily from Easter to late September. Steam days with train rides last Sunday in each month and Bank Holidays.

Before Britain's railways were taken into state ownership in 1948, each region had its own railway company. Among the best known were the L.M.S. – London Midland & Scottish, and L.N.E.R., London North Eastern Railway. But perhaps the best loved was the G.W.R. Officially, it was the Great Western Railway, but ask anyone in the south west, and they will tell you with pride that it was really 'God's Wonderful Railway.'

When Isambard Kingdom Brunel was asked to build a railway, he determined to make it the best in the world. By 1841, the line from London to Bristol was complete, and trains ran on his broad gauge track until 1892. There is a reconstruction of the track at Didcot, where they are also reconstructing his first Fire Fly Steam Locomotive dating from 1839.

The age of Brunel was the age of steam, but sadly, it passed into history when diesel took over in the 1960s. Since then, railway enthusiasts all over the country have formed societies to preserve the romantic traditions of steam. The Great Western Society is dedicated to preserving the Brunel tradition at their Railway Centre in Didcot, where there's plenty to do and see for all ages. Visitors can ride on beautifully-restored trains of the 1930s, and see them coaled and watered just as they were in the old days. They have even re-created a country railway station complete with a working signal box. Special Steam Days are held throughout the year, when great steam giants are put through their paces. With Thomas the Tank Engine Days for the children, and special photographer days, there's always something to interest the family.Admission for adults is from £3 to £5 depending on the event; but there are reductions for children and the over 60s. There's also a good Souvenir Shop, and Refreshment Room.

For further information telephone Didcot (01235) 817200.

The first locomotive purchased by the G.W.R. Society at Didcot. No.1466, 0-4-2 T auto tank, 48XX class built in Swindon.

No.5029, 'Nunney Castle', 4-6-0 Castle class general express locomotive built at Swindon, 1934.

HARPSDEN

BARN DECORATION OF WALLPAPER BLOCKS

Location:	Opposite the Village Church.
Access:	No public access, but the barn can be viewed from the road.

The barn at Harpsden Court Farm, opposite the village church, is well worth the visitor's attention. Though it stands on private property to which there is no public access, its end wall faces the road from where it can easily be viewed. What makes this barn so interesting is the wide variety of hand-carved wallpaper pattern blocks, used to decorate the wall.

The blocks were acquired towards the end of last century by Mr. John Noble of Park Place, Remenham. He bought them from a London printing works, with the intention of using them to line the walls of his boathouse, but died before it could be done. They were stored for some time in the stables at Park Place, before being brought to Harpsden Court. There are other buildings on which wallpaper pattern blocks have been used in this way, a fine example being on the front of several houses in Drybridge Street, near the old Monnow Bridge at Monmouth.

WANTAGE

UNUSUAL KNUCKLE-BONE PAVING

Location:	Stiles Almshouses on Newbury Street.
Access:	The almshouses are not open to the public and permission to view should be sought.

Though not unique, the knuckle-bone paving at Wantage is certainly unusual. Carefully preserved on either side of the covered main entrance to Stiles Almshouses, it is a good example of a kind of paving once quite common. Though the Wantage paving is constructed from the knuckle-bones of sheep, bones from deer, goats and other animals were often used. It has been suggested that the bones of sheep were used at Wantage because of the abundance of sheep on the nearby downs, where they were raised to provide sheepskin for the local glove making industry. There are numerous examples of similar paving. In 1869 The Builder magazine recorded bone paving in Broad Street, Oxford, which was '. . . laid with trotter bones in a pattern of squares arranged angle wise within a border.' The floor of a cockpit at Eton was laid with sheep knuckle-bones, which were supposed to provide a good footing for the fighting cocks.

A plaque above the main entrance to the almshouses records the gift of Robert Stiles, a Merchant of Amsterdam, who died in 1680. Little seems to be known of Robert, but Stiles was a common name in Wantage, and he was probably a native of the town. In 1645, at the age of twenty, having been apprenticed to a London draper, he went to Amsterdam. Before leaving, he made a will in which his belongings were listed as: clothes, a table, thirty shillings and the goods his father gave him. When he died thirty-five years later, he left an estate worth £150,000.

WANTAGE

ALFRED THE GREAT – KING AND WARRIOR

> *Location:* Market Place.

Most people remember Alfred the Great as the King who burnt the cakes. It is a legend that seems to have outlived his many other great achievements. Until recent years, it was still perpetuated in Wantage, where pupils of the local Grammar School served burnt cakes to their guests on their annual speech day. The statue of the West Saxon King in the town's Market Place, commemorates his nobler achievements. Sculptured in Sicilian marble by Queen Victoria's nephew Prince Victor of Hohenlohe Langenburg, it depicts the King with a battleaxe in one hand, and parchment scroll in the other. A bronze plaque on the base records:

ALFRED the GREAT
The West Saxon King
Born At Wantage A.D.849

Alfred found learning dead and he restored it.
Education neglected and he revived it.
The Laws powerless and he gave them force.
The Church debased and he raised it.
The land ravaged by a fearful enemy from which he delivered it.
Alfred's name will live as long as mankind shall respect the past.

The statue was unveiled by the Prince and Princess of Wales in 1877. The Prince, later crowned King Edward VII was a direct descendant of Alfred. Perhaps sensitive to the Danish-born Princess of Wales, no mention is made by name of Alfred's defeat of her fellow countrymen.

UFFINGTON

TOM BROWN'S SCHOOLDAYS MUSEUM

Location: Uffington Village.

Access: Tom Brown's School Museum is open to the public from Easter-
October at weekends and Bank holidays: 2pm-5pm, and other
times by arrangement. Tel: 01367-820402 or 820631.

'Our village was blessed among other things with a well-endowed school. The building stood by itself, apart from the master's house, on an angle of ground where three roads met; an old grey stone building with a steep roof and mullioned windows.' This is the village school at Uffington, as described by Thomas Hughes in his enchanting novel, *Tom Brown's Schooldays*. Tom, being the son of the local squire didn't go to the village school, but he was encouraged by his father to make friends with the local lads, who attended the school.

Tom was educated privately, and as his lessons finished earlier than those of the village schoolboys, he went to the school to await his friends. It was often a long wait, and impatient, Tom peeped at the boys through the school door; much to their amusement, and the annoyance of the master who frequently chased him off. He did it once too often and was caught. But you must read the book for yourself to find out what happened to Tom.

The old school building still stands at the cross-roads, but it isn't a school anymore. Uffington now has a larger village school, which seems to be thriving when sadly, so many have closed. The old school is now a Tom Brown Schooldays Museum filled with interesting relics of village life. The rules of the school are still on the wall, and are a salutary reminder of what it was like in *Tom Brown's Schooldays.*

The author of *Tom Brown's Schooldays* was born at Uffington, where his father was rector. For some years, the village was also home to the much loved poet, Sir John Betjeman, who was a churchwarden there.

UFFINGTON

THE GREAT WHITE HORSE

> *Location:* White Horse Hill: can be reached along the Ridgeway on foot or by car.
>
> *Access:* Open daily throughout the year – National Trust.

The White Horse, above Uffington, must be one of the most intriguing landmarks in Britain. Its strange elongated shape can be seen galloping across the downs, from several vantage points, long before you reach White Horse Hill. It is perhaps best viewed from a distance, but for those wishing to see it at close quarters, there is a good road onto the hill with ample parking for cars.

Shrouded in myth and legend, the origin of the White Horse has always been subject to considerable speculation. Some say it was cut out to celebrate King Alfred's defeat of the Danes. Others attribute it to the same period as nearby Uffington Castle, built by Celtic tribesmen about the 2nd or early 1st century B.C. In more recent years, the folk around Uffington, have preserved their pre-historic heritage, by periodically scouring the monument to keep it white. Always a cause for celebration, the story of the 1857 scouring is colourfully told by local author Thomas Hughes, in his book *The Scouring of the White Horse*. Scouring lasted two days, and was a festive occasion for a family day out with some spirited merrymaking. The high spot was the pig race in which thirty runners pursued a pig over White Horse Hill. *The Reading Mercury* reported thirty thousand people present at the 1780 scouring. Among the many attractions were cart horse races, 'ridden by carters in smocks without saddles.' 'A good hat to be run for by men in sacks.' 'A flitch of bacon to be run for by asses.' 'A cheese to be run for down the White Horse Manger.' and 'A jingling match by eleven blindfold men, one unmasked and hung with bells, for a pair of buckskin breeches.' They certainly knew how to enjoy themselves in the old days.

At the foot of White Horse Hill is a large mound known as Dragon Hill, where Saint George is said to have slain the dragon.

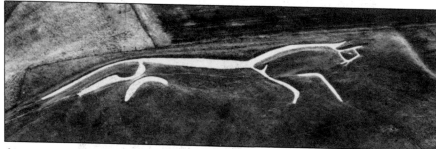

(Courtesy of English Heritage Picture Library)

KINGSTON LISLE

THE BLOWING STONE

Location: Outside Blowing Stone Cottages on the Lambourn road at Kingston Lisle.

The Blowing Stone is a large boulder, three feet high by three feet wide. It is full of holes that are thought to have been made by tree roots. Though not classed as an ancient monument, it is doubtless very old. Its origins seem to be lost in antiquity and legend, and it has clearly been an important part of local folklore for a very long time. According to local tradition, King Alfred, summoned his troops by blowing the stone:

> *'The Bleawin Stwn in days gone by*
> *Wur King Alfred's bugle harn.'*

It is mentioned in *Tom Brown's Schooldays*, when the stone stood outside a local pub known as 'The Blowing Stone' or Blawin Stwun as the locals call it. 'What's the name of your hill, landlord?' 'Blawin Stwun Hill, sir, to be sure.' 'And of your house? I can't make out the sign.' 'Blawin Stwun, Sir.' says the landlord . . . 'What queer names!' 'Bean't queer at all, as I can see, Sir, says mine host . . . , 'seeing as this here is the Blawing Stwun his self . . . Like to hear un Sir?'

The stone now stands in the front garden of Blowing Stone Cottages. There isn't a landlord to blow it now, but you might be lucky enough to persuade one of the children who live there to show you how it is done. They are particularly adept at blowing the stone, and produce a lovely deep fog horn sound.

ASHBURY

WAYLAND'S SMITHY

Location:	On the Ridgeway – well signposted.
Access:	Open daily – English Heritage.

If you are unacquainted with this part of Oxforshire, the signposts pointing to Wayland's Smithy, might suggest a local version of Gretna Green. You won't find a blacksmith's shop; but there is a magnificent ancient burial chamber made of enormous sarsen stones. There has been a burial chamber here since New Stone Age people occupied this hill-top site more than 5000 years ago. The original tomb was lined with wood, and contained the remains of about fifteen people. A new and much larger tomb was later built above it, completely hiding the original. The new chamber is thought to have been used for several centuries before being sealed. In 1920, the site was excavated, and the remains of eight people found.

Saxons settled here, and named the tomb after Wayland, their magical god. In his youth, he was apprenticed to metal craftsmen known as the Trolls. The apprentice's skill soon surpassed the skill of his mentors, so that noblemen and even kings were proud to possess his work. Wayland was kidnapped by the Swedish King Niduth, and held in a cave. He retaliated furiously by killing the king's two sons whose skulls he made into a pair of goblets which he presented to their father. When the king's daughter visited the captive smith to have a ring repaired, Wayland attacked and raped the unfortunate princess. He finally fled to freedom on a pair of wings he had made, taunting the king as he went. Thereafter, he lived in caves, and according to legend, would shoe the horse of any passing traveller who left a silver penny by the tomb that now bears his name.

BIBLIOGRAPHY

Adair, John	*A Life Of John Hampden The Patriot 1594-1643*
Anderson, J.R.L.	*The Upper Thames*
Blackwood, John	*Oxford's Gargoyles and Grotesques*
Blanchflower, Garth	*The Bridge at Henley on Thames*
Bloxham, Christine	*Portrait of Oxfordshire*
Bond, J. Gosling, S & Rhodes, J.	*Oxfordshire Brickmakers*
Burton, Anthony	*Shell Book Of Curious Britain*
Dufty, A.R.	*Kelmscott – An Illustrated Guide*
Green, David	*Blenheim Palace Guide*
Grinsell, L.V.	*The Blowing Stone*
Harris, Molly	*Where The Windrush Flows*
Hibbert, Christopher & Edward	*The Encyclopaedia Of Oxford*
Hughes, Thomas	*Tom Brown's School Days*
Hughes, Thomas	*The Scouring of the White Horse*
Lethbridge, Richard	*Shell Guide – Oxford & Berkshire*
Maharajah's Well Trust	*Maharajah's Well – Illustrated Guide*
Mee, Arthur	*The King's England – Oxfordshire*
Miller, Edith	*History of Islip*
Oxford University Press	*The Victoria History of the County of Oxford*
Peddie, John	*Alfred – The Good Soldier*
Potts, William	*Banbury Cross & The Rhyme*
Rees, David	*The Son of Prophecy*
	Henry Tudor's Road to Bosworth
Renshaw, Peter	*A Guide To The Memorials & Brasses of Ewelme Church*
Seymour, William	*Battles In Britain 1066-1547*
Sherburn, George (Ed.)	*Correspondence of Alexander Pope*
Soames, Mary	*The Churchill Family Album*
Stubbings, N Rhodes, J & Mellor, M	*Oxfordshire Potters*
Tames, Richard	*William Morris*
Yurden, Marilyn	*Shire County Guide Oxfordshire*

THE AUTHOR

Born in Manchester, Edward Gill has lived most of his life in the country since leaving the city for Shropshire as a wartime evacuee. He has spent much of the past forty years in the Cotswolds and the Welsh Borderland, where he developed a particular interest in Monmouth, about which he has written and broadcast. In 1987, his book, *Nelson and the Hamiltons On Tour,* was published. It tells the fascinating story of Nelson's triumphant tour in the summer of 1802, from the home he shared with the Hamiltons in Surrey, through Oxford and Gloucester to South-west Wales and the Midlands. The author has motored more than 1½ million miles in the course of his business, and has used the opportunity to explore many varied and interesting places he has encountered along the way.

S.B. Publications publish other titles in this series.
For details write (enclosing S.A.E.) to: S.B. Publications, c/o 19 Grove Road, Seaford, East Sussex BN25 1TP.

Bale tombs, Burford Parish Church.